DRED SCOTT

RESOLVING THE MYTH OF A COLOR-BLIND CONSTITUTION

by

Larry Kenneth Alexander

Copyright © 2023 by Larry Kenneth Alexander

All rights reserved. No part of this publication may be reproduced, distributed, or transmitted in any form or by any electronic or mechanical means without the prior written permission of the publisher/author, except in the case of brief quotations embodied in critical reviews and certain other noncommercial uses permitted by copyright law.

Printed in the United States of America

ISBN: 979-8-9891501-0-6

Contact author at lalexander@metroworksusa.com; (651) 325-8436

Contents

BRITANNIA AND THE SOUTHERN COLONIES TIMELINE . i
FORWARD 1
INTRODUCTION 4
THESIS 5

I. HISTORY OF SLAVE LAWS AND NEGRO RESOLUTIONS DURING COLONIAL TIMES 6

    HUB AND SPOKE CONSPIRACY 22

    HISTORICAL BACKGROUND 31

    DRED SCOTT DECISION 47

    EXAMINATION BEFORE THE COMMITTEE OF THE WHOLE OF THE HOUSE OF COMMONS, 13 FEBRUARY 1766 59

II. HISTORY OF THE COLOR-CONSCIOUS CONSTITUTION 127

III. BLACK ENGLISHMEN OF EQUAL SOCIAL AND POLITICAL RELATIONS 137

IV. VIRGINIA'S COLONIAL ASSEMBLY COULD NOT ENACT A SLAVE LAW 140

V. THE IMPERIAL GOVERNMENT ABOLISH DEFECTIVE COLONIAL LAWS 144

VI. THE JAMES SOMERSET HABEAS CASE 160

VII. AMERICA'S DECLARATION OF INDEPENDENCE 169

VIII. AMERICA'S REVOLUTION AND SLAVERY 178

VII. THE TREATY OF PARIS OF 1783 200

VIII. THE CONSTITUTION REVEALED 205

CONCLUSION 222
END NOTES 237

BRITANNIA AND THE SOUTHERN COLONIES TIMELINE

100,000 years ago   Nigritic Africans migrated to the Americas by way of Bering Strait.

10,000 years ago   Cheddar Man thrived in England. He's a hunter gatherer who had dark brown skin, blue eyes, and Negroid features.

7,000 years ago   Aboriginal black Native Americans migrated to the Mississippi Valley region of the southern United States.

43 AD   The Roman Empire conquered England.

410 AD   Roman rule ended in England.

1215   King John signed Magna Carta which prohibited slavery in England and guaranteed justice for all under the rule of law throughout the British Empire.

1328   King Edward the Third married a woman of Moorish descent... Queen Phillipa. She's England's first black Queen consort.

1526   Enslaved Africans were part of a Spanish expedition to establish an outpost on the North American coast in present-day South Carolina.

1586   Scores of Africans plundered from the Spanish were aboard a fleet under the command of Sir Francis Drake when he arrived at Roanoke Island, Virginia.

1606	King James the First granted the first charter to the colony of Virginia and it memorialized that the colony will be bound by England's rule of law and the Magna Carta. Born in Virginia conferred British subjecthood per charter and all legal rights of being an Englishman.
1616	Africans in the West Indies were at work in Bermuda providing expert knowledge about the cultivation of tobacco.
1619	The first nineteen Africans are brought to Point Comfort, Virginia in British America. The rule of law officials made Africans indentured servants and after a proscribed period each was granted freedom and British subjecthood. Their children were born Englishmen.
1632	The colony of Maryland was granted a charter and it memorialized that the colony was bound by England's rule of law and the Magna Carta. Born in Maryland conferred British subjecthood.
1638	The New England slave trade begins in Boston.
1640	The legislative assembly of Virginia enacted a law that excluded lacks from the requirement of possessing arms.
1661	The Parliament of Great Britian enacted the *Sedition Act of 1661* criminalizing the passing of laws in the Kingdom by inferior legislatures without first securing England's King's assent.
1662	The legislative assembly of Virginia enacted a law of *partus sequitur ventrem*: chattel slavery. Any child born to an enslaved woman will also be a slave. It

	violated parliamentary law setforth in the *Sedition Act of 1661*.
1663	In Gloucester County, Virginia, the first documented slave rebellion in the American colonies took place.
1663	The colony of Maryland legalized slavery without the King's Assent.
1664	The legislative assemblies of Virginia, Maryland, New York, New Jersey, and the Carolinas each passed a law that mandated lifelong servitude for black slaves without the King's Assent.
1676	The British created the "white race" in response to Bacon's Rebellion in Virginia where all classes within colony rebelled against British rule.
1667	The legislative assembly of Virginia enacted a law that baptism does not bring freedom to blacks.
1668	The legislative assembly of Virginia enacted a law that free black women, like enslaved females over the age of 16 are taxable. White women remained nontaxable.
1669	The legislative assembly of Virginia enacted a "casual killing of slave" law that if a slave dies while resisting his master, the act will not be presumed to have occurred with "prepended malice."
1672	The legislative assembly of Virginia enacted a law that it is legal to wound or kill an enslaved person who resisted arrest. Owners of any slave killed as he resisted arrest would receive financial compensation for the loss of an enslaved laborer.

1680	The legislative assembly of Virginia enacted a law that it now legal for a white person to kill an escaped slave who resisted capture. Slaves are forbidden to:

- arm themselves for either offensive or defensive purposes. Punishment: 20 lashes on one's bare back:
- to leave the plantation without the written permission of one's master, mistress, or overseer:
- "[to]… lift up his hand against any Christian." Punishment: 20 lashes on one's bare back.

1682	The legislative assembly of Virginia enacted a law that made imported Africans——slaves for life without the King's Assent.
1689	England's Parliament enacted Bill of Rights. The bill codified the liberty rights of all Englishmen. No Englishman can be born a slave.
1691	The legislative assembly of Virginia enacted a law that any white person married to a black or mulatto is banished and could not stay in colony for more than three months after they are married.

- A mulatto child born to a white indentured servant would serve a 30-year term of indenture.
- A fine of 15 pounds sterling was levied against white women who gave birth to mulatto children. And if a woman could not pay the fine, she was condemned to serve five years as an indentured servant.

1692	The legislative assembly of Virginia enacted a law that slaves are denied the right to a jury trial for capital offenses. They also legislate that enslaved individuals are not permitted to own horses, cattle, and hogs after December 31of that year.
1702	England's Court of the King's Bench ruled in *Smith v. Browne & Cooper* that "as soon as a negro comes to England, he is free; one may be a villein [serf] in England, but not a slave."
1705	The legislative assembly of Virginia enacted a law that declared all non- Christian servants entering the colony to be slaves. It defined all slaves as real estate; acquitted masters who killed slaves during punishment; forbade slaves and free colored people from physically assaulting white persons and denied slaves the right to bear arms or to move abroad without written permission.

- Determined that if a white man or white woman married a black partner, the white individual would be sentenced to jail for six months and fined 10 pounds current money of Virginia.
- Determined that any minister who married an interracial couple would be assessed a fine of 10,000 pounds of tobacco.
- Determined that any escaped slave who was unwilling or unable to name his or her owner would be sent to a public jail.

1708	The Southern colonies required militia captains to enlist and train one slave for every white soldier.

1708	Blacks outnumbered whites in South Carolina.
1712	The New York Slave Revolt of 1712. The American colonies restricted the importation of Africans into their colonies and encouraged domestic slave practices.
1729	The colonies of South and North Carolina were granted charters and each memorialized that the colony would be bound by England's rule of law and the Magna Carta. Born in either colony conferred British subjecthood per charter and all legal rights of being an Englishman.
1732	The colony of Georgia was granted a charter and it memorialized that the colony as bound by England's rule of law and the Magna Carta. Born in Georgia conferred British subjecthood and all legal rights of being an Englishman.
1735	Georgia's Assembly enacted slavery laws within the colony without the King's Assent.
1739	Slaves in Stono, South Carolina rebelled, sacked and burned an armory and killed whites. The militia put an end to the rebellion.
1751	King George II specially repealed Virginia's Slave Code of 1705.
1761	King George the Third married Sophia Charlotte, daughter of Duke Charles Louis Frederick of Mecklenburg- Strelitz——Queen Charlotte. Descendant of the black branch of the Portuguese Royal House. Under America's Black Codes——she's black and due to their interracial marriage Virginia's 1691 law outlawed the King and Queen.

1762	Queen Charlotte gave birth to George the Fourth, who upon birth was named the Prince of Wales; the heir apparent to the British throne. Under America's Black Codes——he's black.
1763	Kingdom of Great Britain abandoned its informal policy of salutary neglect.
1764	Parliament enacted the *Stamp Act of 1764*. Riots and civil unrests erupted within the American colonies opposing the act.
1765	Parliament convenes to consider repealing the *Stamp Act*.
1766	Parliament repealed Stamp Act and passed the *American Colonies Act of 1766*, commonly known as the *Declaratory Act of 1766*.
1770	Crispus Attacks, a black Englishman was the first person to die in Boston Massacre.
1772	A unanimous ruling in *James Somerset v. Charles Stewart*, King's Bench, June 1772 by England's Twelve Judges that slavery was not "allowed and approved by the laws of this Kingdom" and can only be lawful by way of "positive law." Slavery was deemed unconstitutional throughout the British Empire and 15,000 native sons are immediately released from bondage in England and Wales.
1774	The First Continental Congress convened in Philadelphia to organize colonial resistance to Parliament's Intolerable Acts passed in May of the same year and vowed to discontinue the slave trade after the first of December.

1775	Lord Dunmore, the governor of Virginia declared martial law and granted freedom for all slaves held in bondage by colonial patriots. However, per English law, all slaves in American colonies are liberated.
1776	England's thirteen colonies declared themselves an independent nation and issued its Declaration of Independence in July. The first three grievances against King George III related to his failure to freely give his "Assent" to laws proposed by colonial assemblies. The First Congress of the U.S. conferred citizenship unto all free Englishmen and formally adopted English rule of law.
1779	England's General Henry Clinton issued The Phillipsburg Proclamation that declared freedom to all Revolutionary War-era slaves and conferred British subjecthood unto Africans suffering as slaves in the American colonies.
1782	The United States sued for peace and preliminary articles of peace are finally agreed to and signed by the parties. England required that all its citizens be "set at liberty" and the United States agreed, as a condition for peace. All hostilities ceased.
1783	Abuses were rampant. Black Englishmen were terrorized by slave catchers, and England filed a formal complaint with the U. S. delegation which included George Washington. The delegation was informed that England took the position that former slaves, those born in colonial America were Englishmen under his Majesty's protection and that

	its practices of assaults and kidnappings had to cease.
1783	General Guy Carleton transported 3,000 black citizens out of the United States. Carleton and the U. S. both in respective registries called Book of Negroes journaled their names and other supporting information.
1784	Congress ratified the Treaty of Paris of 1783——but failed to release 500,000 black citizens, relegated them to slavery claiming black people are legal property of white Americans. The United States violated its first international treaty.
1787	Delegates convened a constitutional convention to draft a new federal United States Constitution.
1787	Congress reached a compromise to have an Electoral College and to count black Englishmen as three-fifths of the number of white inhabitants of that state for legislative and taxing purposes.
1788	Congress ratified the United States Constitution.
1790	Congress denied naturalization to anyone who is not a free white.

Dedication

To my sister Maynet, who reminded me that words have the power to change the world.

FORWARD

In July 2023, Sons and Daughters of the Enslaved (SADE), a nonpartisan, tax-exempt, public policy and educational organization, launched a Review of the U.S. Constitution to offer an evidence-based and nonpartisan analysis of whether the U.S. Constitution is color-blind or whether it is color-conscious in ratifying denials of fundamental due process of established legal protection to 500,000 black Englishmen entitled to liberty and freedom under the *Treaty of Paris of 1783*. To address the bold scope of this project, we have complemented our in-depth research with the U.S. Supreme Court's *Dred Scott* decision of 1857—the law of the land. While this book responds to the pressing constitutional questions of the day, it seeks to construct long-term solutions that will inform the public, and political decision-makers and to advance the on-going debate.

England's "free society" came to tolerate slavery only because it was distant and across the ocean. The only forced labor recognized was feudal *villeinage*. In 1587, Hector Nunez complained to the Court of Requests that he had "no remedie ...by course of the Common Law of this realme... to compell" an 'Ethiopian' who "utterly refuseth to tarry and serve' him to serve him during his life." No statutes codifying modern slavery were ever enacted in the Kingdom of Great Britain.

England's common law rejection of slavery on its sovereign soil—while its colonies, although legally bound by colonial charters to the same English common law—enacted pretended slave laws have continued to plague the substantive debate within the Anglo-Saxon jurisprudential community over the legality of slavery within the British Empire during the 17th and 18th centuries for countless decades.

The government of the United States, a former British colony, and each of the 13 States joined the Anglo-Saxon jurisprudential community in July 1776 and did so—over delegate Thomas Jefferson's strident objection. This Congressional act fastened this nation and each State to the English common law—a precedent-based system and all parliamentary laws. This included the *Declaratory Act of 1766* abolishing all statutes, resolutions, votes, orders, proceedings, and laws enacted by colonial assemblies in the American colonies in 1766 that "denied" the power and authority of Parliament to enact binding laws within the American colonies or if they violated parliamentary laws. England's common law decisions, and most famously the *James Somerset v. Charles Stewart* decision in 1772, became the law of the land.

In June 1772, four years *before* independence was declared—Lord Chief Justice Mansfield in the *Somerset* decision observed in delivering the unanimous verdict of the Twelve Judges of the Court of the King's Bench—one, that slavery was an institution so "odious" and so contrary to the natural law that it could exist only by statute—a "positive law." Unless a positive law established the slave relation, slavery had to be assumed not to exist. In the absence of such a statute in England, the slave relation had to be considered of no effect in that country, and two, slavery was not approved and allowed in the Kingdom based upon American statutes and Laws.

It was based upon the *Somerset* decision that caused a Missouri circuit court to grant an enslaved African American named Dred Scott and his family their freedom in 1850. However, hearing the case on appeal, the Missouri Supreme Court reversed the circuit court's decision and declared Scott and his family still enslaved. According to that court, the relevant law was that prevailing in Missouri, not in Illinois or the Wisconsin Territory, present-day Minnesota.

The case eventually made its way to the U.S. Supreme Court, wherein, in a 7-2 decision, the Court ruled against Scott. The U.S. Supreme Court Chief Justice Roger B. Taney found that although some states extended citizenship to blacks, under the terms of the U.S. Constitution, blacks were not... and never could be... citizens of the United States. Further, Taney wrote blacks were "regarded as beings of an inferior order, and altogether unfit to associate with the white race, either in social or political relations; and so far inferior, that they had no rights that the white man was bound to respect." Because Scott was not a U.S. citizen, stated Taney, he was not entitled to bring suit in the U.S. Supreme Court, and so the Missouri Supreme Court's decision against him stood.

INTRODUCTION

The *Atlantic* article... *How Conservatives Turned the 'Color-Blind Constitution' Against Racial Progress*, the writer Theodore R. Johnson posed the question... "Does the Constitution care about race? Or, put another way, is the Constitution color-blind?" [1] The United States Supreme Court has long since answered that question negatively with the *Dred Scott v. John A. Sandford*, 60 U.S. 393 (1857) decision.

The Supreme Court's analysis in *Dred Scott* of the Framers' original intent reveals that a "perpetual and impassable barrier was intended to be erected between the white race and the one they had reduced to slavery." [2] The *Dred Scott* decision, in effect, determined the Constitution is not "color-blind" with its findings that the Declaration of Independence never intended to include or acknowledge "the class of person who had been imported as slaves nor their descendants," and "the negro might justly and lawfully [be] reduced to slavery for his benefit,"—which is still "good law."

The Supreme Court is charged with the power to interpret the U.S. Constitution. The *Dred Scott* decision prevents conservatives from weaponizing the post-*Dred Scott* aspirational framing of the U.S. Constitution as a color-blind instrument since "the Framers drafted the three-fifths compromise as a means to delineate enslaved black Americans and Native Americans from the rest of the citizenry."

Color-Blind Constitution

Moreover, as the writer Johnson stated, "In the same year that the last state ratified the Constitution, Congress passed, and George Washington signed the *Naturalization Act of 1790*, which reserved citizenship exclusively for "free white persons" of good character."

Furthermore, the ratification of the U.S. Constitution was color-conscious,[3] even though the Framers did not mention race since 500,000 Revolutionary War-era black Englishmen under the English rule of law, entitled to be "set at liberty" under the *Treaty of Paris of 1783* were denied the fundamental right to due process of law and summarily made the bedrock of America's slave-based economy upon this replacement Constitution's ratification. The *Dred Scott* decision has determined the question and has resolved the myth of a color-blind constitution.

THESIS

The U.S. Constitution is not a color-blind document in contemplation, construction, or effect, as it ratified the denial of due process protections to 500,000 legally free black colonials and approved slave ownership claims of America's Founding Generation.

I. HISTORY OF SLAVE LAWS AND NEGRO RESOLUTIONS DURING COLONIAL TIMES

England's *Magna Carta of 1215*, Article 39, provided as follows:

"No freemen shall be taken or imprisoned or disseised [sic] or exiled or in any way destroyed, nor will we go upon him nor send upon him, except by the lawful judgment of his peers or by the law of the land."

The British Constitution was not a written document with specific rules and laws; it embodied English common laws and customs passed down from the *Magna Carta of 1215* through the ages of history. [4] In the seventeenth century, the English common law became an instrument to create new laws in the form of new precedents, and common law was an avenue England's monarch could use to expand its power and to legitimate slavery. Common law is a precedent-based system often characterized as conservative, local, and relatively unchanging. The modern term is *stare decisis* or the idea that courts uphold prior decisions or precedents.

The rule of law was perfected in England with the birth of Parliament, dated *circa* 1265. The power and authority of Parliament are inextricably linked to the doctrine of parliamentary supremacy and parliamentary sovereignty. The extent of the "power and authority" of the Parliament is encapsulated within the principle of

Parliamentary sovereignty," according to noted scholar A. V. Dicey, it "means neither more nor less than this, namely that Parliament thus defined has, under the English constitution, the right to make or unmake any law whatever, and further, that no person or body is recognised [sic] by the law of England as having a right to override or set aside the legislation of Parliament." [5] The vesting of this power and authority in Parliament was because it was seen as a repository of the highest and most absolute power of the English Kingdom to which everyone was linked, from the King to the humblest of subjects. [6]

Parliament passed the *Royal Assent by Commission Act* in 1541 and, in 1661, the *Sedition Act of 1661*. The substance of these two acts of Parliament was to prevent individuals and other lesser legislative bodies from purporting to enact laws within the Kingdom of Great Britain by requiring the assent of England's King unto all pretended resolutions, votes, orders, or proceedings as a requirement to be considered a proper pronouncement of a statute or law within the Kingdom. All thirteen English colonies within British North America were granted a charter after 1541. Each grantee and its lawgivers of each colony agreed to secure the Assent of England's King upon all portended resolutions, votes, orders, and proceedings its colonial assembly might advance in progressing such legislation to become a colonial statute or law.

In 1619, when the first nineteen or twenty kidnapped Africans arrived in colonial Virginia, the lawgivers in Virginia applied the law of the land, explaining why the original Africans became indentured servants—not slaves.

Indentured servitude was brutal and deadly... many people died well before their terms were over. But indentured servitude was temporary, with a beginning and an end, typically six to nine years. Afterward, these Africans, no different from other immigrants, became British subjects when they completed their term of indenture. Thus, these original Africans became members of the political community formed and brought into existence by the Constitution. They were treated no differently than other colonists, who served as indentured servants in America.

Further, history supports that these Africans were then eligible for headrights for land in the new colony in the Chesapeake Bay region, where indentured servants were more common. All children, including the children of the original Africans born within colonial America, were born free British subjects and had legal rights and privileges under parliamentary law. Slavery was never legal in colonial America and began and operated extrajudicially.

No English person could be born a slave, and being born in colonial America made the person a freeborn Englishman with an unalienable right to liberty under England's *Bill of Rights of 1689* and colonial charter. Their British subjecthood was also based upon

England's common law doctrine of *jus soli* and colonial charter, and England's King protected all children.

While colonial assemblies could and did make some separate codes, those codes could not be "repugnant" or contradictory to English law. They had to conform to it. Further, all colonial laws had to be approved by royal governors with strict instructions from the king and *Privy Council*, and each colonial charter required the assent of England's King. Virginia's colonial charter also significantly provided for a bicameral legislative structure with England's King, headed by a colonial governor. Virginia's colonial assembly—the *House of Burgesses*, had no legislative power or authority to legalize slavery or to pass colonial resolutions, votes, orders, and proceedings without first acquiring the assent of the imperial government.

The Parliament of Great Britain strengthened the law regarding the King's assent unto colonial statutes and laws by passing the *Sedition Act of 1661*. This parliamentary law made it a treasonous offense to suggest or promulgate "a legislative power without the king." Thus, the rule of English law created a significant legal challenge to Virginia's hereditary slave statutes, laws, and slave resolutions from becoming lawful, which began the following year in 1662 in the colony of Virginia.

Mindful of the fact that slavery at birth within colonial America was not allowed and approved under the English rule of law and it violated parliamentary law,

Virginia's *House of Burgesses*, its colonial assembly, pretended to enact a hereditary resolution called *partus sequitur ventrem*, which purported to change the patrilineal descent law of *partus sequitur patrem* for people of African ancestry in 1662. The colony of Virginia's colonial resolution provided:

"WHEREAS some doubts have arisen whether children got by any Englishman upon a negro woman should be slave or free. Be it therefore enacted and declared by this present grand assembly, that all children borne in this country shall be bond or free according to the condition of the mother."

The hereditary slavery resolution of *partus sequitur ventrem* decreed in the colony of Virginia that children of mothers with African ancestry would be born into slavery, regardless of the English rule of law of *partus sequitur patrem* and the colonial charter that conferred English subjecthood and legal rights to all born on British soil—*jus soli*. The speciousness of Virginia's colonial resolution is quickly revealed since, under the English rule of law, there was no legal condition of being a slave or "bond" recognized throughout the Kingdom of Great Britain. Furthermore, this colonial resolution did not have the weight of being a law since the colony of Virginia did not have the assent of England's King and violated the *Sedition Act of 1661*, parliamentary law. [7]

Normally—Virginia's hereditary slavery law could have been appealed to the *Privy Council* through Virginia's high court; however, Virginia's governor was in criminal league with its colonial assemblymen, and they foreclosed any judicial review of this the hereditary slavery resolution targeting colonial-born people of African ancestry in the colony of Virginia. [8] The language of judicial review that is still used in the United States today, that State laws and court decisions cannot be repugnant to federal law or Supreme Court precedent, was already the norm in the seventeenth century. Colonial slavery within the American colonies emerged outside the imperial legal system.

Subsequently, the other twelve colonies within colonial America followed Virginia's *House of Burgesses's* model. In consort and agreement, these colonial assemblies throughout British America institutionalized and exported hereditary slavery throughout the Kingdom of Great Britain by corrupting colonial governments—using graft and pronouncements of legislative resolutions in derogation of their colonial charters, and all violated various parliamentary laws.

The significance of the failure of colonial assemblies to secure formal approval of England's King upon its hereditary slavery resolutions and slave laws within the American colonies is dispositive—especially since all legislation that targeted colonial-born black Englishmen after Parliament passed the *English Bill of Rights of 1689* was doubly problematic as they undermined England's *Magna Carta of 1215* and as well as questioned parliamentary law. Parliament's legislation in 1689 made it plain that hereditary slavery resolutions and slave laws, which relegated black colonials below the rule of English law, were colonial tyranny and a criminal scheme.

The imperial government was not supervising or enforcing the rule of English law within the American colonies—as it had an unofficial policy of salutary neglect when it came to colonial governance and tacitly granted its colonial assemblies self-rule—but that came to an end in 1763 when George Grenville became the Prime Minister of the Kingdom of Great Britain.

Minister Grenville directed Parliament to pass the *American Revenue Act of 1764,* commonly called the *Sugar Act,* which decreased the taxes from the earlier 1733 tax but was more harshly enforced. This meant more revenue for England. Also, if the Americans broke the law by smuggling in sugar or molasses or not paying the required taxes, they would be tried by a Vice-Admiralty Court. These military courts did not have juries and were less forgiving than general courts.

Americans saw the new *Sugar Act* as a replacement for the earlier act—not a way to make money. Furthermore, as the *Sugar Act* decreased taxes and supplemented it with more criminal enforcement, there were few complaints in most of the colonies. However, throughout the New England colonies, it was a different story, and it led to significant resistance, where manufacturing rum was a big industry.

Samuel Adams of the colony of Massachusetts led the first protest of the *Sugar Act* in Boston. Adams tried influencing the local government and even got many merchants to boycott British goods. Boycotting became a tool Americans used to protest. A committee of five members called the *Committee of Correspondence* was chosen in June 1764 in Massachusetts to coordinate written communications with other colonies, and it had little success in rallying other colonies.

Concerning the *Currency Act of 1764*, during the 1700s, "bills of credit" were typically used by governments in the colonies to represent silver or gold coins. This was because silver and gold were scarce in the colonies. Bills of credit made trade easier—but cut the British out of the transaction because they were using gold and silver. British merchants refused to be paid in bills of credit and demanded compensation in hard currency—gold and silver. The *Currency Act* prohibited the printing and issuing of paper money by colonial assemblies.

Further, Americans could no longer use bills of credit in official trades. The British imperial government wanted more control over their economy and established fines and penalties for members of colonial assemblies who disobeyed despite the long-standing currency shortage. However, the *Currency Act of 1764* did not cause wide-spread protests in the American colonies. The British imperial government had banned printing colonial currency in certain territories in earlier years. Many Americans saw this act as an extension of those earlier parliamentary laws.

On November 1, 1765, Parliament's *Stamp Act* became the law of the land within the American colonies despite months of protests. The *Duties in American Colonies Act of 1765,* commonly known as the *Stamp Act,* was enacted by Parliament on March 22, 1765, which required colonists to pay taxes on every page of printed paper they used. The tax also included fees for playing cards, dice, and newspapers. [9]

The reaction within the American colonies was immediate. The Americans argued that only a representative legislature had the legal authority to tax the American colonies under the rule of English law. The Americans claimed—that taxation was unconstitutional as no representatives from the American colonies served in Parliament. That summer, the colony of Massachusetts called for a meeting of all the colonies—the *Stamp Act Congress*—to be held in the colony of New York in October 1765. *Committees of Correspondence* were also formed in the colonies to coordinate protests against the *Stamp Act.*

In the colony of Virginia, its colonial assembly— the *House of Burgesses,* was forwardly opposing the *Stamp Act of 1765* and proffered a resolution against the act. The *Virginia Resolves* has originally five resolves, which stated that all people in a colony have the same, equal rights to everything that a man born in the realm of England has the rights to. Further, two rejected resolves were subsequently printed and circulated throughout the colonies by Virginia's delegate, Patrick Henry, and one of them stated Virginians were not bound by any laws that did not come from its own legislative body. With little doubt, a colonial loyalist speedily forwarded delegate Henry's resolve to Parliament.

Moreover, in a speech before the House of Burgesses, the newly-elected delegate Patrick Henry threatened the King with retaliation if the taxes were not immediately revoked, treasonous words. With only a few attendees, the Virginia body was the first colonial assembly to reject the *Stamp Act*.

Eight other colonial assemblies followed Virginia's lead. They passed similar resolutions to that of Virginia, and soon, the *Stamp Act Congress* convened in New York to address the concerns of the several colonial assemblies and agreed to send to Prime Minister Grenville and King George III its agreed-upon resolution titled *The Declaration of Rights and Grievances*. Further, it had fourteen points that went beyond addressing the *Stamp Act*, laid out that while intending to remain subordinate to Parliamentary authority, the American colonies expected the liberties understood within the English Constitution to be afforded to them, too.

On August 14, 1765, outrage boiled over in Boston. Protestors organized as the *"Sons of Liberty"* took to the streets defiantly against British rule—carrying the effigy of Andrew Oliver, the city's stamp tax agent, and placing him before the *Liberty Tree* near Boston Common. Soon, a mob of several thousand people attacked Oliver's office and home, and the effigy was stomped, decapitated, and burned.

The Stamp Act Congress's *Declaration of Rights and Grievances* caused shock, bewilderment, and anxiety. Grenville tried to mend the warring forces by reassuring the King and parliamentary opponents that the colonies were not coordinating to act against his authority. But the damage had been done. Grenville's ministry collapsed. On his way out, Grenville scowled and reaffirmed that the American colonies must obey Parliamentary authority or else. His successor, Lord Rockingham, who was pro-American, asked Dr. Benjamin Franklin of the colony of Pennsylvania to testify before the House of Commons on February 13, 1766, as they debated and considered repealing the *Stamp Act*—he agreed. One month after Franklin's testimony—the *Stamp Act* was repealed.

Simultaneously, Parliament enacted the *American Colonies Act of 1766*, commonly called the *Declaratory Act of 1766,* on March 18, 1766. In the words of a contemporary observer, the intention of the *Declaratory Act* "was to stifle all differences by the establishment of an undeniable principle" that Parliament had the constitutional power to legislate the American colonies in case the repeal of the *Stamp Act* should leave anyone with the mistaken belief that it had given that up.

The *Declaratory Act* had plain wording, and it forcefully proclaimed three main things:

- That the colonial assemblies did not have the *sole* and exclusive right to impose duties and taxes upon their colonial subjects.

- That Parliament had "full power and authority to make laws and statutes of sufficient force and validity to bind the colonies and people of America... in all cases whatsoever," just as it had in Britain.

- And any laws or resolutions made by the colonial assemblies denying Parliament's rightful authority to make laws governing them were repealed and made utterly null and void.

Exultant Americans celebrated the repeal of the *Stamp Act* across the colonies—church bells were rung—festive galas were given, and days of public rejoicing were held. While Americans perceived the *Declaratory Act of 1766* as an attempt to save face and a vacuous law—this act of Parliament fundamentally altered colonial governance within the American colonies. [10] The *Declaratory Act* had legislatively rendered all "resolutions, votes, orders, and proceedings" enacted by colonial assemblies "utterly null and void" if they "denied" or "questioned" parliamentary law in the American colonies "in all cases whatsoever," which colonial hereditary slavery resolutions and related colonial slave fiats did.

Years passed. On December 3, 1771, members of the *Society for the Abolishment of Slavery* headed by Londoner Granville Sharp petitioned His Majesty's

Court of the King's Bench—its highest court and Lord Chief Justice Mansfield of that court for habeas corpus relief for a colonial-born enslaved Black person named James Somerset, who was confined in irons aboard a slave ship heading for Jamaica on orders of American enslaver Charles Stewart.

Somerset was living in London, and he ran away on October 1, 1771, and was hunted in London and captured, where he was placed on the slave ship *Ann & Mary,* commanded by Captain John Knowles. Somerset was heading for hard labor in the Jamaican sugar fields—an assured death sentence.

Lord Chief Justice Mansfield of the Court of the King's Bench issued a writ of habeas corpus and so began the case of *James Somerset v. Charles Stewart* and the judicial review of colonial American slave laws. [11] Mansfield did everything he could to pressure a settlement so that this legal question could remain unanswered. Frustrated, as he and his wife cared for his young bi-racial grandniece Belle in his home and sensitive to the optics—*sua sponde,* Mansfield impaneled Twelve Judges tribunal for a solemn decision.

Significantly, this judicial review of colonial American slave laws concluded with a unanimous ruling of the twelve judges that found: "The state of slavery is of such a nature that it is incapable of being introduced on any reasons, moral or political, and instead, only by positive law, which preserves its force long after the reasons, occasion, and time itself from whence it was created is erased from memory. It is so odious that nothing can be suffered to support it but positive law. Whatever inconveniences, therefore, may follow from a decision, I cannot say this case is allowed and approved by the law of England, and therefore, the black must be discharged." [12]

By positive law, England's Twelve Judges was referring to an act of Parliament and, by so doing, was affirming parliamentary sovereignty over the American colonies. This unanimous ruling of the Court of the King's Bench became the law of the land in the Kingdom of Great Britain, which included the American colonies in 1772. All black colonials suffering as enslaved people within the American colonies became legally free people, as their liberty rights were restored because of the English rule of law. Slavery in colonial America could only be a lawful condition if authorized by a "positive law," a legislative power that only Parliament possessed: parliamentary sovereignty.

In July 1776—after the Founding Fathers declared independence, the U.S. Congress fastened this new nation to the rule of English law by formally adopting Anglo-Saxon jurisprudence and the English common law over delegate Thomas Jefferson and others' strong objections. Jefferson advocated for a clean break from the Kingdom of Great Britain and its common laws in July 1776. He and his followers wanted Congress to adopt Roman law, perhaps recognizing that this would offer the U.S. the best chance to reconcile its colonial hereditary slavery practices and their ultimate ownership claims of 500,000 colonial blacks—which the *Dred Scott* decision summarily ratified in 1857.

Based upon Parliament's abolishment of all hereditary slave resolutions, votes, orders, and proceedings on March 18, 1766 which violated parliamentary laws, and the *Somerset* decision in 1772 that slavery was not "allowed and approved" by the laws of the Kingdom of Great Britain, colonial America's slavery practices were outlawed and abolished—Jefferson's failure to have the U.S. Congress supplant the English rule of law is highly significant as it had the legal effect and consequence of conferring unto all black colonials living in the American colonies the same liberty rights and legal status as white colonials on July 4, 1776.

Furthermore, every State government in the U.S. specifically enacted a reception statute, adopting Anglo-Saxon jurisprudence and the English common law before the American Revolution ended—fastening all State governments to the rule of English law. Functionally and legally, by adopting the English rule of law—England's *Magna Carta of 1215* and England's common law decisions regarding slavery such as *Somerset v. Stewart* (1772)—*Smith v. Brown & Cooper* (1701) and *Smith v. Gould* (1706), which ruled—the common law did not recognize blacks as different to other people and conferring due process rights unto all black colonials under the *Magna Carta of 1215*—they became the law of the land throughout the United States.

Color-Blind Constitution

Inexplicably—the U.S. Supreme Court in *the 1857 Dred Scott v. John A. Sandford* case ignored the U.S. Congress's adoption of the rule of English common law, the *Somerset* decision in 1772, and Parliament's *Declaratory Act* of 1766, which rendered colonial slave "resolutions, votes, orders, and proceedings" "utterly null and void," in 1766 because they violated parliamentary laws. Further, *Dred Scott* opinion was 55 pages long, and most of those pages were dedicated to answering its misapprehended threshold legal question of whether Scott, as a descendant of black enslaved people, had the legal standing to sue in federal courts.

Taney relied upon a flawed rendition of history and Thomas Jefferson's vocation as a slave owner to conclude that when he wrote that "all men were created equal" in the Declaration of Independence, he only referred to white men. This was wholly problematic and a mistaken approach. Further, Taney mistakenly framed the threshold legal question for Dred Scott as "Can a negro, whose ancestors were imported into this country, and sold as slaves, become a member of the political community formed and brought into existence by the Constitution of the United States, and as such become entitled to all rights and privileges, and immunities, guaranteed by that instrument to the citizen? "

Instead, the threshold question that confronted the U.S. Supreme Court in *Dred Scott* in 1857 was vastly different, as it was... Did the Parliament of Great Britain nullify all colonial America's resolutions, votes, orders, and proceedings that denied or questioned parliamentary laws and thereby abolished colonial America's slavery resolutions and slave laws and did so by way of the *Declaratory Act of 1766* and the *Somerset* decision since the U.S. Congress adopted the English rule of law after declaring itself a new nation in July 1776, which made Scott a member of the political community formed and brought into existence by the Constitution of the United States?

HUB AND SPOKE CONSPIRACY

England's Twelve Judges, impaneled as the Court of the King's Bench by Lord Chief Justice Mansfield, struck down the practice of colonial American slavery in *Somerset v. Stewart* in June 1772. One of the eleven other judges who was elevated from the Court of Common Pleas to hear this case was William Blackstone, the author of one of the most famous legal texts ever written, *Commentaries on the Laws of England*. In 1765, in the *Commentaries* about slavery, he wrote… "And this spirit of liberty is so deeply implanted in our constitution, and rooted even in our very soul, that a slave or a Negro, the moment he lands in England, falls under the protection of the laws and so far becomes a freeman."

It was the following year, in 1766, that the Parliament abolished all hereditary slave "resolutions, votes, orders, and proceedings" and slave laws enacted by the 13 colonial assemblies since these inferior legislative assemblies within colonial America were violating various parliamentary laws and the *English Bill*

Color-Blind Constitution

of Rights of 1689. Furthermore, even the Declaration of Independence's grievance section, redress number 21, indicted the imperial government and King George III "For taking away our Charters, *abolishing our most valuable laws*, and altering fundamentally the Forms of our Governments." The *"most valuable laws"* abolished and which the Founding Fathers complained about in the Declaration were their hereditary slavery laws.

Revisionist historians, in their long-standing defense of colonial slavery within the American colonies—argue that slavery predates written human records, and people were enslaved in almost every ancient civilization. However, in all those instances—slavery manifested the sovereign's will and authority. Slavery within the American colonies was not a manifestation of the will and authority of Great Britain's monarch or its imperial government. No statutes codifying modern slavery ever passed in England. Instead, slavery came to colonial America due to criminal behavior—a hub-and-spoke conspiracy never allowed and approved by the King of Great Britain or by a positive law enacted by Parliament.

The "hub-and-spoke conspiracy" in colonial America had three parts—a hub (Virginia's *House of Burgesses*)—spokes (the 13 American colonies), and a rim (white colonials). Essentially, it was a series of separate vertical agreements between a central actor, who is one level of the supply chain or mastermind—the hub, and co-conspirators on a different level of the supply chain or scheme—the spokes, and a horizontal agreement among the spokes to the same scheme that each spoke reached individually with the rim. Further, it came to be the first time in human history that a race of oppressed people came to oppress another group because of racial differences, in violation of the law.[13]

The criminal conspiracy of colonial slavery involved wealthy planters in the colony of Virginia in the late 1650s and early 1660s, pretending to enact the hereditary slave resolution *partus sequitur ventrem*. This criminal scheme made colonial-born people of African ancestry slaves at birth. Further, these planters conspired and teamed with Virginia's colonial lawmakers, who purported to pass resolutions, votes, orders, and proceedings without the requisite legislative power and authority. Under the English rule of law, no legal condition was recognized as "slave." Virginia's hereditary law was also in legal conflict with England's common law doctrine of *partus sequitur patrem*, which declared that the legal condition of a child born in the colony of Virginia was defined patrilineally by the child's father's condition.

Moreover, the conspirators had a secret weapon, colonial governor Berkeley. The governor should have vetoed this hereditary slave resolution because it violated the colonial charter and the English rule of law. However, he benefitted from this scheme, and he, in his capacity, foreclosed legislative review by the *Privy Council* and higher judicial review to the Court of the King's Bench in London.

The scheme was void *ab initio* as the hereditary slave resolutions did not have the King's assent and violated parliamentary law. The passage of time did not make such colonial resolutions valid, and thus, the question of whether slavery was ever lawful must be analyzed and resolved based on the rule of English law.

Under the British rule of law tradition, a government official's actions only have the force of law when the person acts within the rule of law. Further, when a government official acts without the imprimatur of any law, he or she does so by sheer force of personal will and power. This, too, was provided for under the English rule of law during colonial times throughout the American colonies. Thus, the hereditary slavery resolutions of colonial government officials authorizing hereditary slavery were never law.

Furthermore, Virginia's colonial governor did not veto the resolution as he was paid to look the other way. Then, he acted as if it was a valid colonial resolution and stopped all legal challenges to this hereditary slave resolution through England's *Privy Council* and the Court of the King's Bench—for profit.[14] Virginia's colonial assembly merely pronounced—hereditary slavery was the law in colonial Virginia, and its acceptance was due to colonial government corruption. Virginia's genetic slave model was copied and adopted by the other twelve colonies. Colonial tyranny, corruption of colonial government, and hereditary slavery became endemic throughout colonial America—lasting over one hundred years due to the British imperial government's unofficial policy of salutary neglect toward the American colonies.

During this time—the Parliament of Great Britain enacted the *English Bill of Rights of 1689*, reaffirming fundamental legal rights guaranteed to English subjects and all others in the realm—reaffirming

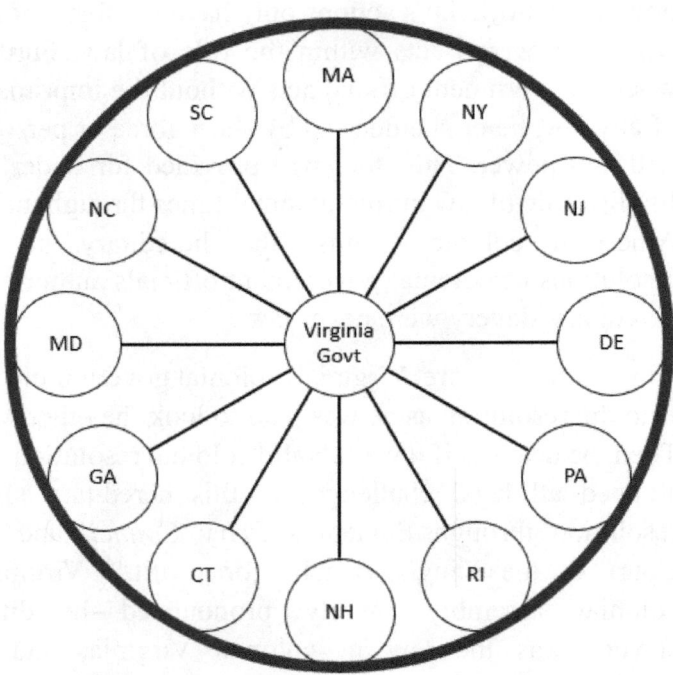

doctrines that were first announced in England's *Magna Carta of 1215, i.e.,* habeas corpus and the prohibition of cruel and unusual punishment.

The imperial government of Great Britain abandoned its informal policy of salutary neglect towards the American colonies in 1763. In 1766—the Parliament enacted the *American Colonies Act of 1766,* also known as the *Declaratory Act of 1766.* The act opened by summarizing the American argument that only colonial assemblies had the right to impose taxes on Americans. However, Parliament countered the American argument by declaring that the colonies were subject to the King and Parliament, who alone had the right to make laws binding on the colonies "in all cases whatsoever."

Further, in section II of the act, Parliament abolished all legislative colonial fiats enacted by colonial assemblies within the American colonies that "denied" or "questioned" parliamentary law, making them "utterly null and void to all in purposes whatsoever," and this legislation was self-executing. [15] The words in the act had a plain meaning. The context was understandable and had the legal effect of legislatively abolishing previously enacted hereditary slave statutes and slave laws passed by colonial assemblies within the American colonies since the extralegal practice of hereditary slavery at birth for colonial-born people of African ancestry was a colonial fiat based upon the colonial resolution of *partus sequitur ventrem.*

The *partus sequitur ventrem* resolutions enacted by colonial assemblies in the American colonies and all resulting colonial slavery statutes and slave laws based upon the extralegal practice denied and questioned the power and authority of Parliament and violated parliamentary laws. These violations of parliamentary laws included the *Royal Assent by Commission Act of 1541*—the *Sedition Act of 1661*—the *Habeas Corpus Act of 1679*, which provided that individuals could not be imprisoned without trial, deprived of habeas corpus, or detained until charged with a crime,[16] and the *English Bill of Rights of 1689* which bolstered these enumerated civil rights. The imperial government's decision not to enforce the act was political and did not impact this legislation as it was self-executing.

The *Declaratory Act of 1766* abolished "all resolutions, votes, orders, and proceedings" passed by colonial assemblies within the American colonies, which denied or questioned Parliament's power and authority over the 13 colonies—parliamentary sovereignty. This parliamentary law responded to riotous protests within the American colonies and Parliament's begrudging decision to repeal the *Stamp Act of 1765*. Parliament had the authority and power to make laws within the American colonies, as parliamentary sovereignty was foundational and well-established throughout the Kingdom and in colonial America.

Britain's *Institute for Government* and *Bennett Institute for Public Policy* published its views on parliamentary sovereignty in 2023, and it noted that Britain "has a predominating political as opposed to a predominating legal constitution, as any limits on parliament's power to enact legislation come from political pressure and not from the law. Parliament may have the power, legally, to enact legislation requiring the slaughter of all blue-eyed babies. However, political pressure means that it would never do so. This pressure comes from the conscience of MPs and the wishes of the electorate." [17] Thus, the threshold issue of whether the Parliament had the authority and power to make any law regarding the American colonies was well-settled.

Parliament recognized that colonial America's economy was robust, lucrative, and successful based upon its century-old hereditary slavery scheme that violated parliamentary laws. Parliament surmised that Americans were overlooking or minimizing the imperial government's unofficial salutary neglect policy, allowing their family and themselves to amass their wealth. Or, if they truly believed—the Parliament had no power to pass a colonial law due to the passage of time, these inferior legislative assemblies were denying and questioning the authority and power of the Parliament; such misapprehensions, beliefs, and impressions needed to be purged within the American colonies.

Moreover, in 1772—Lord Chief Justice Mansfield of England's Court of the King's Bench in *James Somerset v. Charles Stewart,* having referred the habeas case for judicial review of its American slave laws to the Twelve Judges procedure, affirmed the doctrine of parliamentary sovereignty and the sole and exclusive power and authority of the British Parliament to enact slave statutes and laws within the Kingdom. First, Mansfield declared slavery was "odious." Second,

Mansfield stated on behalf of the tribunal—slavery was not "allowed and approved by the laws of this Kingdom." Third, slavery within the Kingdom could only be legal if authorized by a "positive law," a legislative power and authority that only Parliament possessed. This *Somerset* decision immediately freed Somerset and 15,000 black Englishmen living in England.

The Americans declared themselves independent of Great Britain four years after the *Somerset* decision in July 1776. Still, the U.S. Congress and all thirteen states—formally adopted the English rule of law and its controlling common law of the *Somerset* decision and other cases such as *Smith v. Brown & Cooper*, where Chief Justice Holt ruled "that as soon as a negro comes into England, he becomes free: one may be a *villein* in England, but not a slave." [18] The U.S. Congress's adoption of the English rule of law and U.S. constitutionalism is binary—locked in mutual orbit with the *Dred Scott* decision in 1857. Further, as the English common law did not recognize blacks as being different from other people in colonial America and the U.S. Congress formally adopted the English common law in July 1776—black Englishmen living in colonial America were included in the Declaration of Independence pronouncement that "all men were created equal," as the *Somerset* decision ruled slavery was not "allowed and approved by the laws of this Kingdom" in 1772.

Furthermore, during the American Revolution, the black colonials were emancipated through British

General George Clinton's *Phillipsburg Proclamation* on June 30, 1779. The legal status of black Englishmen became controversial after the *American Revolution* ended with the *Treaty of Paris of 1783* when British General Guy Carleton claimed liberty for all black colonials and America's General George Washington, and he could not agree on whether black Englishmen must be "set at liberty" under the treaty in May of 1783.

This international dispute concerning the liberty rights of black Englishmen was an international incident, and in having adopted Anglo-Saxon jurisprudence and England's common law and both generals agreeing to have their governments address the matter—the U.S. was legally obligated to give each Revolutionary War-era black held as a slave in the United States a due process hearing. However, 500,000 black Englishmen were denied the fundamental right to due process of law—enslaved and became the bedrock of America's slave-based economy—ratified in the U.S. Constitution.

HISTORICAL BACKGROUND

In *Dred Scott*, Supreme Court Chief Justice Taney ruled that African Americans were not citizens of the United States, and banning slavery meant depriving owners of their property without due process of the law violated the Fifth Amendment of the U.S. Constitution. This inference from Taney was particularly ironic, considering the property at stake were descendants of 500,000 human beings denied due process of the law, which relegated themselves and their progeny to that of being human property without due process rights—hereditary slavery.

Hereditary slavery emerged extralegally during colonial times outside the British imperial legal system. Hereditary slavery within America was ratified by the U.S. Constitution, as 500,000 black Englishmen were placed outside the rule of law—denied due process of law because of their ethnicity—made the bedrock of America's slave-based economy. [19] This hub-and-spoke conspiracy called hereditary slavery began during the early 1660s in the colony of Virginia—based upon a hereditary slave resolution called *partus sequitur ventrem*—in the absence of the King's approval and abolished by Parliament's *Declaratory Act of 1766*—parliamentary law. Hereditary slavery, a criminal scheme, became endemic throughout the British American colonies due to graft, racial tyranny, and widespread corruption of colonial government officials.

History confirms the English monarchy endorsed slave-trading initiatives in the 1560s with Queen Elizabeth I's support of John Hawkins' slave expeditions. Hawkins raided African settlements on the West African coast and seized hundreds of enslaved captives from Portuguese ships in three separate voyages backed by government officials, London merchants, and the queen. Then, during the reign of King Charles II, from 1660 to 1685—the Crown and members of the royal family invested heavily in the African slave trade. Seeking to bolster the restored monarchy's wealth and power and supplant the Dutch in the Atlantic trading system, Charles granted a charter to the *Company of Royal Adventurers Into Africa*, a private joint-stock company—less than six months after ascending the throne.

More generally, the courts under King Charles II and James II, as under their father, Charles I, had often allowed English Kings to circumvent Parliament, ignore laws, and effectively create new ones. Courts became such crucial instruments of absolutism that after the revolution against James II in 1688, the revolutionary *"Convention Parliament"* that met in the spring of 1689 purged and punished all twelve high court justices of the common courts and decreed that no decisions from James II's reign should ever be cited as precedent.

During the peak years of the African slave trade, between 1690 and 1807, European enslavers carried approximately 6 million enslaved Africans to the Americas—almost half of these captives arrived in British or Anglo-American ships. The production of popular, labor-intensive agricultural products such as sugar, tobacco, cotton, and coffee in the Atlantic colonies hinged on the regular supply of African captives. Most enslaved African men, women, and children were destined for the sugar fields of Brazil and the Caribbean islands. Protected by the Crown and Parliament, the slave trade became Britain's most profitable enterprise.

Future readers must understand that hereditary slavery within colonial America is distinguished from the *Atlantic Slave Trade* since the rule of English law prohibited the practice and never authorized slavery on British soil. Further, during the late 17th century and the beginning of the 18th century, harsh new slave codes or negro laws limited the rights of people of African descent. They cut off their avenues to freedom within the American colonies. [20]

Additionally, Virginia's colonial assembly in 1691 prohibited colonial slaveholders from emancipating enslaved blacks unless they paid for the freemen's transportation out of the colony of Virginia, [21] and this colonial assembly began condemning mixed-race children of free white women to serve as indentured servants for thirty years. It also subjected the mother to a fifteen-pound sterling fine. As punishment for having a mixed-race child, the mother would be indentured for five years—if she failed to pay the ascribed fine within a month of the birth. [22] The colony of Virginia also criminalized interracial marriage in 1691,[23] and subsequent Virginian laws abolished free blacks' rights to vote, hold office, and bear arms.[24]

Virginia's colonial assembly, as historian Betty Wood, in her book *Origins of American Slavery,* observed that the colony of Virginia codified and systematized slave laws in 1705. Wood continued, noting, "[T]hese laws would be modified and added to over the next century and a half, but the essential legal framework within which the institution of slavery would subsequently operate had been put in place." [25] However, all things equal—Virginia's colonial slave legislation

Color-Blind Constitution

and all slave laws throughout the American colonies were all legislatively abolished by section II of Parliament's *Declaratory Act of 1766*. Verbatim, the other twelve American colonies adopted these so-called "slave laws" and employed the same organizing tactics as the colony of Virginia to establish hereditary slavery. They were void *ab initio* since they exceeded the legislative authority granted to each colonial assembly within the American colonies based upon their colonial charter. All such colonial proceedings authorizing slavery "denied" or "questioned" the power and authority of Parliament to make binding laws in the American colonies as they violated parliamentary laws and were automatically rendered "null and void" by the *Declaratory Act of 1766*.

Virginia's colonial assembly conflated its hereditary slavery scheme with the *Atlantic Slave Trade* narrative to mask its unlawfulness. Hereditary slavery practices were wildly outside the English rule of law, and slave-holding colonists relentlessly cultivated the image of benevolent, civic-minded, and law-abiding. Revolutionary War-era blacks were enslaved people under colonial traditions and properly promulgated laws.

Under Parliament's *Royal Assent by Commission Act of 1541*, the English King's formal assent was required to enact a valid law or resolution throughout the Kingdom. Still, none of the colonial assemblies within the American colonies adhered to this parliamentary law. Moreover, in 1661, Parliament passed the *Sedition Act of 1661*—this parliamentary law criminalized the utterance of pretended laws by petty government officials who might utter a law or resolution without the assent of the imperial government. The scheme of pretending to enact valid slave statutes, resolutions, or slave laws in colonial America victimized countless people of African ancestry and denied them due process of law.

Furthermore, this lower house of Virginia's bicameral colonial legislature—Virginia's *House of Burgesses* failed to secure the assent of England's King on pretended colonial legislation. This was criminal, however, draped with the adornment of lawfulness and being positioned as being a codified law, and aided by the Royal Governor of Virginia and others—the practice of chattel slavery brought wealth and power to these lawbreakers, and the course became widespread throughout colonial America. Graft, corruption of colonial government officials, and colonial tyranny targeted against people of African ancestry prevailed.

The British imperial government rebounded, and it asserted parliamentary sovereignty by way of the *Declaratory Act of 1766,* which legislatively abolished all colonial "resolutions, votes, orders, and proceedings" that "denied" or "drawn into question" the power and authority of the Parliament.[26] All colonial legislative fiats concerning slavery were rendered null and void and returned everyone in colonial America suffering as enslaved people to the status *quo ante* under the English rule of law since they violated parliamentary laws.

Further, there were no limits upon the lawmaking powers of Parliament during colonial times, [27] except it could not enact legislation that would bind a future Parliament, either regarding the content of legislation or how legislation was enacted. Moreover, if any parliament attempted to do so, it would always be possible for a future parliament to reverse this requirement. Such was the principle of parliamentary sovereignty as it existed throughout colonial times.

The British imperial government's highest judicial tribunal—the Court of the King's Bench—after referring the case to the Twelve Judges procedure and then conducting a judicial review of American slave laws—found all colonial slave statutes and laws in the American colonies defective and legislatively deficient in authorizing a legal state of slavery. The tribunal ruled slavery was not "allowed and approved by the laws of this Kingdom," and slavery could only be lawful in the Kingdom by a "positive law" in 1772. Only Parliament had the power and authority to enact a "positive law" in the Kingdom of Great Britain.

Four years later, in July 1776—the *Continental Congress* announced the separation of the 13 North American British colonies from Great Britain. In the Declaration, they substantially abandoned the contention of independence based on the rights of Englishmen; instead, the Declaration put forth the fundamental doctrines of natural rights and of government under social contract. Claiming that Parliament never indeed possessed sovereignty over the colonies and that the crown of right exercised it only under contract, the declaration contended that King George III, with the support of a "pretended" legislature, had persistently violated the agreement between himself as governor and the Americans as the governed. The Founding Fathers proffered a long list of accusations to prove this contention. The 56 Founding Fathers then invoked the right and duty of revolution.

Few can soberly claim that this U.S. government arose among men as the Founding Fathers said it did, and the social contract theory has lost support among political scientists. Further, from a British viewpoint, the Parliament and crown could not be separated, and the histories of the colonies after 1607 were not entirely consistent with the assertion that Parliament had never, as of right, possessed sovereignty over them. Moreover, it could not and was not a compelling argument supporting the legality of hereditary slavery during colonial times, as each colonial legislature was bicameral with England's King. Moreover, a colonial resolution legalizing hereditary slavery mandated the crown's assent under each colonial charter, and all colonial assemblies within the American colonies breached their contractual obligations with England's King by ignoring this jurisdictional requirement during colonial rule.

Furthermore, contractually, each of the 13 colonies within North America was also bound by England's *Magna Carta of 1215* and the English rule of law. Hereditary slavery practices within colonial America violated fundamental Anglo-Saxon jurisprudential doctrines, England common law, and the Court of the King's Bench rulings in *Smith v. Brown & Cooper* (K.B. 1701) and *Smith v. Gould* (K.B. 1706) where Lord Chief Justice Holt ruled there could not be an action of trover in the case of an enslaved Black person, because the common law did not recognize blacks as different to other people. Although blacks could be bought and sold as chattels in Barbados, that was not the case in England.

Moreover, Lord Chief Justice Holt ruled in 1701 that "as soon as a negro comes into England, he becomes free; one may be a *villein* in England but not a slave." The Court meant that a person enslaved in the colonies was not recognized as a slave by English law and was treated with the limited rights of a *villein*: that is, slave-owners still had a right to service when they brought slaves to England from the colonies, but the slave was not their chattel, and he could not be treated as such. Such explains why the original 19 kidnapped Africans who arrived in Virginia in 1619 were treated as indentured servants—not slaves.

In 1750, Baron Thompson in *Galway v. Cadee* (K.B. 1750) followed Holt in declaring that a slave became free on arrival in England, and in *Shanley v. Harvey*, Lord Chancellor Henley stated that as soon as a man sets foot on English ground—he is free. He also asserted that a black slave could take his master to court for cruel treatment. He had a right to a habeas corpus hearing, which protects an individual from arbitrary imprisonment if restrained of his liberty. Despite adopting Anglo-Saxon jurisprudence and England's common law over Jefferson's strong objections in July 1776—the U.S. Congress under the *Articles of Confederation* of 1777 failed to provide a habeas corpus hearing to the 500,000 black colonials, and so did each of the thirteen States after the Revolutionary War in violation of the *Treaty of Paris* and the rule of law. In the *Dred Scott* decision, Taney ignored this legal travesty or misapprehended this controlling law and these common law cases concerning Scott.

Significantly, in *R. v. Stapylton* (K.B. 1771), Lord Chief Justice Mansfield heard a criminal case of assault involving a putative slavemaster, Robert Stapylton, who physically attempted to send a black back to the colonies. The jury concluded that there was no evidence that Stapylton had property in Thomas Lewis. Still, during the trial, Mansfield remarked to Lewis's counsel, John Dunning, that he would prefer the question to remain unsettled because he feared the consequences if slave masters were to lose their property by accidentally bringing their slaves to England. The current historical consensus is that English common law was somewhat confused. *Somerset v. Stewart* (K.B. 1772) solemnly changed the law in imperial Britain as Lord Mansfield submitted the *Somerset* habeas case to its Twelve Judges procedure the following year.

James Somerset was born in colonial Virginia around 1741. When he was eight years old, he was bought by Charles Stewart to serve as his manservant, and he traveled among the northern American colonies, moving to Boston in 1764 and relocating to London in 1768. On October 1, 1771, Somerset left his master's house and refused to return. After two months, he was captured by slave hunters and, on Stewart's orders, delivered to the custody of one John Knowles, captain of the slave ship *Ann & Mary*, where he was confined in irons and bound for sale in Jamaica. Abolitionists working on Somerset's behalf petitioned Chief Justice of the King's Bench, Lord Mansfield, for a writ of habeas corpus. Eventually, his case attracted the attention of the prominent abolitionist Granville Sharp.

Slavery within the British colonies developed extralegally based upon colonial resolutions, votes, orders, and proceedings in derogation of their colonial charters. Significantly, in the mid-seventeenth century, Virginia's colonial assembly, the *House of Burgesses*, passed a hereditary slave resolution of *partus sequitur ventrem*, changing the patrilineal descent system in the colonies to matrilineal.

Somerset's case was immediately seen as a test of the legality of slavery in England. While the colonial planters campaigned for a decision that would recognize colonial laws relating to slavery and enforce them in the metropole, Granville Sharp advocated a ruling that would forbid slavery in England. Thus, when Lord Mansfield held that James Somerset of Virginia was a free man "though the heavens may fall" and cited Sir John Holt's court decisions, the imperial government stopped northern colonial assemblies, such as the Massachusetts colony, from applying the *Somerset* case rulings in the American colonies—the fear of renewed transatlantic tensions was a legitimate concern.

In 1772, the *Somerset* case created anxiety and dissonance within the American colonies. The political machinations of the imperial government caused northern patriots, such as Samuel Adams and John Hancock, to clamor loudly that this evidenced Britain's blithe disregard for the rule of law, proving British imperial governmental tyranny.

In Massachusetts, several slaves had filed freedom suits based upon the *Somerset* decision, and two successive Royal governors vetoed legislative action of the *Massachusetts General Court* to liberate slaves in 1773 and 1774. Although slaveowning Englishmen in the colony of Virginia, such as George Washington, Thomas Jefferson, John Marshall, and others, were pleased with England's policy in the aftermath of the *Somerset* decision—these Virginians believed that this crisis was orchestrated and planned by the British imperial government to rob them of their wealth created from hereditary slavery.

When Jefferson wrote the Declaration of Independence, he sought to harmonize this new nation's ideal of all men being created equal by continuing hereditary slavery and the enslavement of all colonial-born black Englishmen. He rationalized that a clean break away from Anglo-Saxon jurisprudence and England's common law was essential and required as the English rule of law and its caselaw regarding slavery was an indeterminate, ambiguous, and equivocal legal landscape of "judge-made law" on the legality of slavery, which overlapped parliamentary supremacy was highly problematic. Thus, it is fair to say Jefferson was distraught and nearly inconsolable when the U.S. Congress fastened America to Anglo-Saxon jurisprudence and the English rule of law after declaring itself independent of Great Britain in July 1776.

Upon the end of the American Revolutionary War—implicated in the *Treaty of Paris of 1783* that ended that war, a legal dispute existed as to whether Revolutionary War-era blacks living in colonial America totaling 500,000 should be "set at liberty." The British imperial government argued that all such people were entitled to a certificate of liberty because of the English rule of law—their status as Englishmen at birth and since their unalienable right to liberty vested *"previous"* to Great Britain and the United States entering this international treaty; they were legally free. British citizenship was also provided for in each colonial charter and the English rule of law. Further, under the English common law doctrine of *jus soli*—being born in colonial America conferred British citizenship at birth, and all Englishmen had legal rights under the *English Bill of Rights*.

Significantly, an unofficial policy of salutary neglect existed regarding the American colonies from 1689 to 1763. Still, all colonial assemblies within colonial America were bound by their colonial charter and the English rule of law during salutary neglect.

However, each colonial assembly violated its colonial charter and parliamentary law since each pretended to enact hereditary slave "resolutions, votes, orders, and proceedings," which led to the pronouncement of legislative colonial fiats proclaiming hereditary slavery was lawful within their colony.

The colonial governors did not veto such laws, and all legal challenges to the colonial hereditary resolution of *partus sequitur ventrem* were discouraged and prohibited. However, the Parliament in March 1766—abolished all legislative fiats authorizing hereditary slavery within colonial America since such colonial legislation "denied" or "questioned" the power and authority of Parliament since they violated parliamentary laws.

Necessarily, all hereditary slavery statutes and slave laws based upon nullified "resolutions, votes, orders, and proceedings" were automatically abolished as an act of Parliament is self-executing. Without regard to the English rule of law—General Washington endeavored to act as if colonial assemblies were not subservient to the Parliament's supreme legislative power and authority during British colonial rule. Such was the putative basis upon which General Washington claimed that white Americans owned black colonials. There was no legal support to bolster Washington's claim as colonial slavery violated each colonial charter.

Secondly, General Washington's claim of ownership of black colonials faltered since the U.S.

Congress and each state government formally adopted the rule of English law and Anglo-Saxon jurisprudence in July 1776. The simultaneous acts of Congress and all state governments within the United States fastened every American to the rule of English law.

Under Anglo-Saxon jurisprudence and England's common law doctrines, the 500,000 black colonials, who were primarily colonial-born, became the bedrock of America's slave pool in the early 1780s. They were entitled to be "set at liberty" and granted a due process hearing under the *Treaty of Paris of 1783*. All colonial "resolutions, votes, orders, and proceedings" that enslaved or denied fundamental liberty rights to these British subjects during colonial times "denied" or questioned Parliament's power and authority to make binding laws. Parliament's *Declaratory Act of 1766* had rendered "utterly null and void" "all resolutions, votes, orders, and proceedings," which did so, and these black colonials were free Englishmen, as such colonial statutes and laws—violated parliamentary laws. [28]

Ultimately, the Twelve Judges rulings in the *Somerset* case—including slavery was not "allowed and approved by the laws of this Kingdom" during colonial times were controlling precedent. Moreover, the Twelve Judges made the solemn determination in the *Somerset* case in 1772—that American slave laws were legally defective and slavery according to colonial American laws possessed no recognition in English law, having never been established in the common law or by statute. Further, Mansfield declared on behalf of the tribunal that the state of slavery in the Kingdom was not lawfully created by the colonial American slave statutes enacted in the colonies of Virginia and Massachusetts. Moreover, Mansfield also found that the state of slavery was so "odious" that it could only be a lawful condition through a "positive law," a legislative authority that only Parliament possessed. Thus, the legal consequence of the *Somerset* decision was that American colonial slave statutes and laws were adjudged legal nullities, leading to Somerset and 15,000 other black Englishmen's freedom.

Additionally, it was significant that on the 30th of June in 1779, the imperial government's *Phillipsburg Proclamation* emancipated all black colonials suffering as slaves throughout the American colonies. The dispositive legal issue was straightforward. However, without regard to the straightforwardness of the legal dispute, controlling legal procedure, and having a legal right to a due process hearing—500,000 black Englishmen were summarily enslaved and made the bedrock of America's slave-based economy. This denial of due process to black Englishmen foreclosed, suppressed, and prevented these putative British citizens from having their voices heard during the constitutional convention process since if adjudged British subjects under the *Treaty of Paris of 1783,* each would have been lawfully eligible to participate in the ratification of America's Constitution during the late 1780s.

Each enslaved black person living in the erstwhile British colonies—now the United States had

English subjecthood by their birth in colonial America—and no white American had a legal basis to claim ownership of black colonials under the English rule of law. Further, in May 1783, Generals Carleton and Washington agreed to refer the treaty dispute to their respective sovereigns for resolution.

Undeniably, General Carleton claimed liberty for black colonials. He argued that each black Englishman was entitled to a due process hearing under the English rule of law and Law of Nations doctrines. Washington claimed all such people were "property" of its citizens based upon its customs during colonial times. No statutes codifying modern slavery were ever passed in England. Further, at the Star Chamber trial of John Lilburne in 1637, a case quoted as follows: "in [1569], one *Cartwright* brought a slave from Russia, and would scourge him, for which he was questioned; and it was resolved that England was too pure an Air for Slaves to breathe in." Moreover, the legal procedure, process, and controlling law for addressing and resolving the fate of these 500,000 black Englishmen were well-settled as the U.S. Congress adopted the English rule of law in 1776.

DRED SCOTT DECISION

On March 6, 1857, in the case of *Dred Scott v. John Sandford*, United States Supreme Court Chief Justice Roger B. Taney ruled on behalf of the majority of the panel of nine justices—African Americans were not and could not be citizens. Inexplicably, Taney wrote that the Founders' words in the Declaration of Independence, "all men were created equal," were never intended to apply to blacks. Pro-slavery judges from the South dominated the Taney court. Of the nine, seven judges had been appointed by pro-slavery Presidents—five came from slave-holding families. The decision was viewed by many as a victory for the Southern "Slavocracy" and a symbol of the power the South had over the highest court.

Concerning the Declaration of Independence, drafted by Thomas Jefferson and adopted by the *Continental Congress* on July 4, 1776—after much editing by anti-slavery delegates and others, fifty-six English subjects declared independence from the Kingdom of Great Britain. They adopted the famous words "all men were created equal" in the second paragraph. They also adopted the ideal of being "a nation of laws, not men" and proclaimed the equality of colonial Englishmen under the English rule of law—and it was not a racial declaration. These words are controlling, as the U.S. Congress formally adopted Anglo-Saxon jurisprudential doctrines and England's common law in July 1776—fastening England's common law unto the 2,500,000 erstwhile Englishmen in colonial America since British subjecthood inured to all colonial-born people without regard to ancestry, making the Founders' "intentions," desires or undisclosed plans for black colonials an irrelevancy under the English rule of law.

"All resolutions, votes, orders, and proceedings" enacted by the colonial assemblies within the American colonies were legislatively nullified by Parliament in

1766 if they denied or questioned Parliament's power and authority to pass statutes and laws binding the American colonies under the *Declaratory Act*. Objectively, all colonial hereditary slavery statutes and their slave laws enacted within the American colonies violated different parliamentary laws, and under the Act—they all became "utterly null and void to all intents and purposes whatsoever."

Then, six years later—the American slave laws were judicially reviewed *sua sponte* by England's Court of the King's Bench in the 1772 *James Somerset v. Charles Stewart* case, which declared slavery was "odious" and could only be lawful in the Kingdom if the practice was enacted by a "positive law," a legislative power and authority that vested exclusively with Parliament—no colonial assembly in America had the power to enact a positive law. All colonial slave laws within the American colonies were struck down by the judicial determination of the Court of the King's Bench in the *Somerset v. Stewart* case—in effect—deeming all American slave laws as being unconstitutional because colonial assemblies within the American colonies lacked legislative power and authority to enact a valid slavery statute or law under the English rule of law. Under the English rule of law, all slavery laws were void *ab initio*, which returned all black colonials suffering as enslaved people within the American colonies to status *quo ante*, as a matter of law.

Moreover, when Jefferson was penning his draft of the Declaration—he and other slave-holding patriots were anticipating that the English rule of law would be supplanted with Roman law by the U.S. Congress, as they knew Anglo-Saxon jurisprudential doctrines and England's common laws, as well as the *Somerset* decision, were hostile to hereditary slavery and slave laws. Further, as American slave laws and negro laws were struck down and, in effect, deemed unconstitutional—and as slavery had ceased being allowed and approved by any laws in the Kingdom on the 4th of July 1776—all slaveholding patriots were criminals and were violating the English rule of law.

Notwithstanding, the Supreme Court in *Dred Scott* zeroed in on this statement in the Declaration "that all men were created equal" and "endowed by their Creator with certain unalienable Rights." If the Founding Fathers intended to include Black people in that declaration while personally enslaving them," Taney reasoned, that would mean that they were hypocrites who "would have deserved and received universal rebuke and reprobation." But Taney found it impossible that these "great men" acted in a manner so "utterly and flagrantly inconsistent with the principles they asserted." So he concluded, instead, that they intended to exclude Black people from the American political community.

Of the two possibilities, grotesque hypocrisy or white supremacy, Taney, writing for most of the Supreme Court, found the latter far more plausible. Still, a third possibility existed, which was that America's Founding Generation did intend to exclude Black people from the American political community—however—the U.S.

Congress barred these "great men" from doing so with its adoption of Anglo-Saxon jurisprudence and England's common law in 1776—which fastened this new nation to the *Somerset* decision in 1772—Parliament's *Declaratory Act of 1766* and England's *Magna Carta of 1215.*

Taney, a former Maryland slaveholder, explained the language of equality and rights "would not in any part of the civilized world be supposed to embrace the negro race, which, by common consent, had been excluded from civilized Governments and the family of nations, and doomed to slavery," The "unhappy black race," he wrote, was "never thought of or spoken of except as property, and when the claims of the owner of the profit of the trader were supposed to need protection."

Most infamously, Taney wrote that blacks were "regarded as beings of an inferior order, and altogether unfit to associate with the white race either in social or political relations and so far inferior that they had no rights which the white man was bound to respect." He also noted that the U.S. Constitution itself took slavery as a given in the fugitive-slave clause and the slave-trade clause, prohibiting Congress to abolish the "Migration or Importation of such Persons" before 1808 and allowing an import tax of up to "ten dollars for each Person." Taney took this as evidence that the country's founding document did not confer on Black people "the blessing of liberty, or any of the personal rights so carefully provided for the citizen."

As an initial matter—concerning the Founders' words in the Declaration, "all men were created equal," it is essential to highlight that slavery within colonial America was extralegal and a criminal enterprise that Virginia's *House of Burgesses* started by using a legally defective hereditary slavery resolution during the early 1660s. Through colonial government corruption, graft, and racial repression—the other twelve colonies adopted Virginia's slavery practice, and it flourished due to the British imperial government's unofficial policy of salutary neglect, which ended in 1763.

Further, in 1766, the Parliament of Great Britain passed the *Declaratory Act of 1766,* which abolished all pretended colonial resolutions, votes, orders, and proceedings that denied or questioned the power and authority of the parliament to make binding laws in the American colonies. All hereditary slavery resolutions and slave laws were rendered "utterly null and void" as they violated parliamentary laws.

Subsequently, in a judicial review of colonial American slave laws, the *James Somerset v. Charles Stewart* case in 1772, the twelve justices of the Court of the King's Bench unanimously declared colonial slave statutes and laws enacted by colonial assemblies within the American colonies were legally defective since they exceeded their grant of legislative authority.

To this point, most legal scholars have improvidently viewed the *Somerset* decision as one of many common law habeas cases; however, the *Somerset* decision should be examined through the prism of a judicial review of American slave laws. The Twelve Judges decided this case—not just Lord Mansfield. Moreover, this tribunal had original jurisdiction, as it involved a black slave, based upon Virginian slavery statutes and laws, and a colonial subject directly challenging colonial America's slavery statutes and being denied of his liberty rights.[29]

While the ordinary course of the appeal of colonial legislation and cases involving colonials was through the King's *Privy Council* and further appeal, if necessary, before the Common law courts—it was not uncommon for a case to be appealed directly to the Common law courts (by-passing *Privy Council*) or directly to England's Twelve Judges Procedure to secure a solemn determination. Moreover, in having original jurisdiction over colonies in the American colonies, a justice of the Court of the King's Bench possessed inherent jurisdiction and could *sua sponte* refer any matter before him to the Twelve Judges of the Common law courts or any case or controversy involving the American colonies.

Lord Chief Justice Mansfield wanted a solemn determination on the question of the constitutionality of slavery under "American slave Laws," however, he did not want to decide the case by himself, and such was the reason why Mansfield remanded and referred the *Somerset* case to England's Twelve Judges procedure. [30] Yet, countless scholarly writings and books have always attributed the subsequent *Somerset* decision of June 1772 solely to Lord Mansfield. This discrepancy was due to an initiative of the imperial government to minimize transatlantic tension, as a Twelve Judges decision was meant to be a conclusive—definitive ruling on whatever issue upon which that tribunal decided.

Positioning of the *Somerset* decision as being Mansfield alone, who was controversial himself since all of London's "tongues were wagging" about how this highly regarded aristocratic person was caring for his black grandniece in his ancestral home—Kenwood House at this time and its endurance speaks to ingenuity and the palatableness of this suggestion within the American colonies. If one prefers Mason's discernment, the unanimous ruling of the Twelve Judges, or four judges, became the law of the Kingdom of Great Britain, and colonial slavery under American laws became "utterly null and void to all intents and purposes whatsoever."

However, in the book *Slavery and Politics in the Early American Republic*, the scholar Matthew Mason made the illuminating observations that Mansfield "after hearing more arguments and then deliberating over a recess he ruled on behalf of the four-judge court... that Somerset should go free," and that he, Mansfield had "explicitly expressed reluctance to decide such a weighty matter involving such fiercely competing interests and with such potential to disrupt property rights." The scholar Mason's discernment regarding a panel of judges were in the tribunal concerning the *Somerset v. Stewart* case supports this writer's core claim that the *Somerset* decision was rendered by a panel of judges—not just Mansfield.

Moreover, Mason's misapprehension of the number of judges on the *Somerset* panel is explainable since there were traditionally four members, including Mansfield, on His Majesty's Court of the King's Bench and the habeas case remained in the originating court. However, the British Twelve Judges procedure required the other eight judges on the Court of Common Pleas and Exchequer to be temporarily elevated to address the Court of the King's Bench once Lord Chief Justice Mansfield referred this important case to the Twelve Judges. Mason's discernment that the Court of the King's Bench presided *en banc* over the *Somerset* case is still a compelling revelation. Thus, the main take away is the conclusion that a panel of judges addressed the judicial review of American slave laws in 1772—not Mansfield alone.

In the article, *Informal Law-Making in England by the Twelve Judges in the late 18th and early 19th Centuries*, legal scholar James Oldham [31] observes that "When a legal question arose about which the trial judges were doubtful, the most sensible course was to reserve the question for discussion with brother judges at the next opportunity, perhaps at the following term." He observed further that judges would also gather intermittently in the chambers of one of the Chief

Justices, in the Exchequer Chamber, or even in the home of one of the judges.

Importantly, as the King's Bench was acting in a judicial review capacity, the twelve justices considering James *Somerset* of the colony of Virginia's case took into account England's common law decisions regarding slavery and laws passed by Parliament affecting Virginia's colonial hereditary slavery laws and, necessarily, the *Declaratory Act of 1766*. Further, Oldham states also that "the deliberations of the twelve judges made substantial contributions to the growth of the law by establishing controlling precedents, interpreting statutes, fixing rule of evidence, and resolving differences of views among the judges and the three common law courts. . . In many ways, the twelve judges had become a *de facto* court of appeals." Thus, the recognized significance of a Twelve Judges decision on the question of colonial slave legislation after Parliament abolished repugnant colonial resolutions, votes, orders, and proceedings, coupled with the *Somerset* decision six years later—best explains why the imperial government saw the value in attributing this historic decision to Lord Mansfield when this was not the case: the imperial government was endeavoring to minimize transatlantic tensions and chaos within the American colonies.

Secondly, the Declaration's grievance section complains that King George III had proven himself a tyrant for "abolishing our most valuable laws." Further, most impactful concerning the Founders' words in the

Declaration, "all men were created equal," is that the U.S. Congress's adoption of Anglo-Saxon jurisprudence and England's common law, over Thomas Jefferson's strong objections in July 1776, upon which each of the thirteen State legislatures followed. This fastened the U.S. to foundational doctrines that rejected the practice of hereditary slavery, such cases as *Smith v. Browne & Cooper*, where Lord Chief Justice Holt of the King's Bench ruled, "As soon as a negro comes to England he is free; one may be a *villien* in England—but not a slave."

Scholars claim that the ruling in *Dred Scott v. John A. Sandford*, 60 U.S. 393 (1857), is the most egregious example in the court's history of wrongly imposing a judicial solution on a political problem. [32] While few can argue against that determination, here remains the overarching issue focused upon the extent of the Supreme Court's analysis, review, and conclusory finding that the Framers of the U.S. Constitution took it as a given that black slavery was a lawful condition, as Taney found... "We think... that [black people] are not included, and were not intended to be included, under the word 'citizens' in the Constitution, and can therefore claim none of the rights and privileges which that instrument provides for and secures to citizens of the United States." Additionally, Taney, in the *Dred Scott* decision, determined that the country adhered to a cultural belief that "the negro might justly and lawfully [be] reduced to slavery for his benefit."

Doubtlessly, in *Dred Scott*, as the words "all men were created equal" are not ambiguous—Taney should have gone no further, yet he did. *Connecticut Nat'l v. Germain*, 112 S. Ct. 1146, 1149 (1992) (ruling in interpreting a statute, a court always turns to one cardinal canon before all others"... "Courts must presume that a legislature says in a statute what it means and means what it says there.") Moreover, and alternatively, the Supreme Court in *Dred Scott* presumably relying upon "original intent," Taney did not proceed any further once the Supreme Court determined that the Framers of the U.S. Constitution took slavery as a given in the 1857 decision. Furthermore, this points to why the *Dred Scott* decision—famously described as a judicial "self-infliction wound," which helped bring on the Civil War.

Dred Scott was born into slavery in Virginia. During his enslavement, he was taken from Missouri, a slave state, to live in Illinois, a free state, and in a federal territory (present-day Minnesota, Wisconsin, Iowa, and parts of the Dakotas) where Congress had made slavery unlawful. Scott claimed that his stay in Illinois and the territory had emancipated him—a common-law doctrine provided that slaveholders who intentionally transported enslaved people into free jurisdictions freed them, regardless of intent. Chief Justice Taney addressed whether "a negro, whose ancestors were imported into this country, and sold as slaves," *Scott*, 60 U.S. at 403, could become a citizen of the United States. See *id.* Taney relied upon original intent analysis to determine that, when the Constitution was adopted, the Framers did not intend blacks to have the potential for citizenship. Taney held:

> "In the opinion of the court, the legislation and histories of the times, and the language used in the Declaration of Independence, show that neither the class of persons who had been imported as slaves, nor their descendants, whether they had become free or not, were then acknowledged as a part of the people, nor intended to be included in the general words used in that memorable instrument." *Scott*, 60 U.S. at 407.

Among constitutional scholars, the *Dred Scott* decision is widely considered the worst decision ever rendered by the Supreme Court. However, it has consistently played a role in American politics and society long after it was supposed to have been made ineffective by the 13th, 14th, and 15th Amendments of the U.S. Constitution because the Supreme Court never overruled it. It has remained a dominating factor in American politics and society because of white supremacy dogma—structural racism and institutional discriminatory practices.

EXAMINATION BEFORE THE COMMITTEE OF THE WHOLE OF THE HOUSE OF COMMONS, 13 FEBRUARY 1766

The *Declaratory Act* of 1766 included a statement of Parliament's authority and legislative superiority over the American colonies and a display of that authority and power in section II of the *Act* that nullified "all colonial resolutions, votes, orders, and proceedings" throughout the American colonies that denied or questioned Parliament's legislative authority and power over the American colonies—parliamentary sovereignty. This section of the Act would have had no meaning or relevancy but for the fact that the colony of Virginia had denied and questioned Parliament by passing the hereditary slave resolution *partus sequitur ventrem* in 1662 and multiple slave laws which, among other acts, violated Parliament's *Sedition Act of 1661* and the *English Bill of Rights of 1689*.

Further, Virginia's hereditary slave resolution was emulated, adopted, and enacted by the other twelve colonies—and became endemic throughout the American colonies due to a hub-and-spoke criminal scheme and flourished during the period of salutary neglect. However, after nearly 100 years of hereditary slavery being practiced—becoming accepted throughout colonial America—the imperial government abandoned its unofficial policy of salutary neglect in 1763. Moreover, in 1764, Parliament passed the *Stamp Act,* and this caused riots and substantial civil unrest within colonial America. The Americans petitioned Parliament to repeal the *Stamp Act of 1764,* which it convened to consider in the fall of 1765.

British Prime Minister George Grenville, who had championed the *Sugar Act* and *Stamp Act*, fell out of power, and King George III replaced him in July 1765. Charles Watson-Wentworth, the Marquis of Rockingham, succeeded Grenville as Prime Minister who was pro-American, and he invited Dr. Benjamin Franklin of the colony of Pennsylvania, who was living in London, to speak to Parliament about the values and policies of the American colonies with respect to the *Stamp Act*. Franklin's examination revealed two major issues: (1) the Americans believed Parliament had no legal right to tax them, and (2) Parliament had no legal authority whatsoever to make any law of any kind regarding the colonies.

The EXAMINATION of Doctor BENJAMIN FRANKLIN, before an August Assembly, relating to the Repeal of the STAMP-ACT, & c.

[1] Q. What is your name, and place of abode?

A. Franklin, of Philadelphia.

[2] Q. Do the Americans pay any considerable taxes among themselves?

A. Certainly many, and very heavy taxes.

[3] Q. What are the present taxes in Pennsylvania, laid by the laws of the colony?

A. There are taxes on all estates real and personal, a poll tax, a tax on all offices, professions, trades and businesses, according to their profits; an excise on all wine, rum, and other spirits; and a duty of Ten Pounds per head on all Negroes imported, with some other duties.

[4] Q. For what purposes are those taxes laid?

A. For the support of the civil and military establishments of the country, and to discharge the heavy debt contracted in the last war.

[5] Q. How long are those taxes to continue?

A. Those for discharging the debt are to continue till 1772, and longer, if the debt should not be then all discharged. The others must always continue.

[6] Q. Was it not expected that the debt would have been sooner discharged?

A. It was, when the peace was made with France and Spain— But a fresh war breaking out with the Indians, a fresh load of debt was incurred, and the taxes, of course, continued longer by a new law.

[7] Q. Are not all the people very able to pay those taxes?

A. No. The frontier counties, all along the continent, having been frequently ravaged by the enemy, and greatly impoverished, are able to pay very little tax. And therefore, in consideration of their distresses, our late tax laws do expressly favour those counties, excusing the sufferers; and I suppose the same is done in other governments.

[8] Q. Are not you concerned in the management of the Post-Office in America?

A. Yes. I am Deputy Post-Master General of North-America.

[9] Q. Don't you think the distribution of stamps, by post, to all the inhabitants, very practicable, if there was no opposition?

A. The posts only go along the sea coasts; they do not, except in a few instances, go back into the country; and if they did, sending for stamps by post would occasion an expence of postage, amounting, in many cases, to much more than that of the stamps themselves.

[10] Q. Are you acquainted with Newfoundland?

A. I never was there.

[11] Q. Do you know whether there are any post roads on that island?

A. I have heard that there are no roads at all; but that the communication between one settlement and another is by sea only.

[12] Q. Can you disperse the stamps by post in Canada?

A. There is only a post between Montreal and Quebec. The inhabitants live so scattered and remote from each other, in that vast country, that posts cannot be supported among them, and therefore they cannot get stamps per post. The English Colonies too, along the frontiers, are very thinly settled.

[13] Q. From the thinness of the back settlements, would not the stamp-act be extreamly inconvenient to the inhabitants, if executed?

A. To be sure it would; as many of the inhabitants could not get stamps when they had occasion for them, without taking long journeys, and spending perhaps Three or Four Pounds, that the Crown might get Sixpence.

[14] Q. Are not the Colonies, from their circumstances, very able to pay the stamp duty?

A. In my opinion, there is not gold and silver enough in the Colonies to pay the stamp duty for one year.

[15] Q. Don't you know that the money arising from the stamps was all to be laid out in America?

A. I know it is appropriated by the act to the American service; but it will be spent in the conquered Colonies, where the soldiers are, not in the Colonies that pay it.

[16] Q. Is there not a ballance of trade due from the Colonies where the troops are posted, that will bring back the money to the old colonies?

A. I think not. I believe very little would come back. I know of no trade likely to bring it back. I think it would come from the Colonies where it was spent directly to England; for I have always observed, that in every Colony the more plenty the means of remittance to England, the more goods are sent for, and the more trade with England carried on.

[17] Q. What number of white inhabitants do you think there are in Pennsylvania?

A. I suppose there may be about 160,000.

[18] Q. What number of them are Quakers?

A. Perhaps a third.

[19] Q. What number of Germans?

A. Perhaps another third; but I cannot speak with certainty.

[20] Q. Have any number of the Germans seen service, as soldiers, in Europe?

A. Yes,—many of them, both in Europe and America.

[21] Q. Are they as much dissatisfied with the stamp duty as the English?

A. Yes, and more; and with reason, as their stamps are, in many cases, to be double.

[22] Q. How many white men do you suppose there are in North-America?

A. About 300,000, from sixteen to sixty years of age.

[23] Q. What may be the amount of one year's imports into Pennsylvania from Britain?

A. I have been informed that our merchants compute the imports from Britain to be above 500,000 Pounds.

[24] Q. What may be the amount of the produce of your province exported to Britain?

A. It must be small, as we produce little that is wanted in Britain. I suppose it cannot exceed 40,000 Pounds.

[25] Q. How then do you pay the ballance?

A. The Ballance is paid by our produce carried to the West-Indies, and sold in our own islands, or to the French, Spaniards, Danes and Dutch; by the same carried to other colonies in North-America, as to New-England, Nova-Scotia, Newfoundland, Carolina and Georgia; by the same carried to different parts of Europe, as Spain, Portugal and Italy. In all which places we receive either money, bills of exchange, or commodities that suit for remittance to Britain; which, together with all the profits on the industry of our merchants and mariners, arising in those circuitous voyages, and the freights made by their ships, center finally in Britain, to discharge the ballance, and pay for British manufactures continually used in the province, or sold to foreigners by our traders.

[26] Q. Have you heard of any difficulties lately laid on the Spanish trade?

A. Yes, I have heard that it has been greatly obstructed by some new regulations, and by the English men of war and cutters stationed all along the coast in America.

[27] Q. Do you think it right that America should be protected by this country, and pay no part of the expence?

A. That is not the case. The Colonies raised, cloathed and paid, during the last war, near 25000 men, and spent many millions.

[28] Q. Were you not reimbursed by parliament?

A. We were only reimbursed what, in your opinion, we had advanced beyond our proportion, or beyond what might reasonably be expected from us; and it was a very small part of what we spent. Pennsylvania, in particular, disbursed about 500,000 Pounds, and the reimbursements, in the whole, did not exceed 60,000 Pounds.

[29] Q. You have said that you pay heavy taxes in Pennsylvania; what do they amount to in the Pound?

A. The tax on all estates, real and personal, is Eighteen Pence in the Pound, fully rated; and the tax on the profits of trades and professions, with other taxes, do, I suppose, make full Half a Crown in the Pound.

[30] Q. Do you know any thing of the rate of exchange in Pennsylvania, and whether it has fallen lately?

A. It is commonly from 170 to 175. I have heard that it has fallen lately from 175 to 162 and a half, owing, I suppose, to their lessening their orders for goods; and when their debts to this country are paid, I think the exchange will probably be at par.

[31] Q. Do not you think the people of America would submit to pay the stamp duty, if it was moderated?

A. No, never, unless compelled by force of arms.

[32] Q. Are not the taxes in Pennsylvania laid on unequally, in order to burthen the English trade, particularly the tax on professions and business?

A. It is not more burthensome in proportion than the tax on lands. It is intended, and supposed to take an equal proportion of profits.

[33] Q. How is the assembly composed? Of what kinds of people are the members, landholders or traders?

A. It is composed of landholders, merchants and artificers.

[34] Q. Are not the majority landholders?

A. I believe they are.

[35] Q. Do not they, as much as possible, shift the tax off from the land, to ease that, and lay the burthen heavier on trade?

A. I have never understood it so. I never heard such a thing suggested. And indeed an attempt of that kind could answer no purpose. The merchant or trader is always skilled in figures, and ready with his pen and ink. If unequal burthens are laid on his trade, he puts an additional price on his goods; and the consumers, who are chiefly landholders, finally pay the greatest part, if not the whole.

[36] Q. What was the temper of America towards Great-Britain before the year 1763?

Color-Blind Constitution

A. The best in the world. They submitted willingly to the government of the Crown, and paid, in all their courts, obedience to acts of parliament. Numerous as the people are in the several old provinces, they cost you nothing in forts, citadels, garrisons or armies, to keep them in subjection. They were governed by this country at the expence only of a little pen, ink and paper. They were led by a thread. They had not only a respect, but an affection, for Great-Britain, for its laws, its customs and manners, and even a fondness for its fashions, that greatly increased the commerce. Natives of Britain were always treated with particular regard; to be an Old England-man was, of itself, a character of some respect, and gave a kind of rank among us.

[37] Q. And what is their temper now?

A. O, very much altered.

[38] Q. Did you ever hear the authority of parliament to make laws for America questioned till lately?

A. The authority of parliament was allowed to be valid in all laws, except such as should lay internal taxes. It was never disputed in laying duties to regulate commerce.

[39] Q. In what proportion hath population increased in America?

A. I think the inhabitants of all the provinces together, taken at a medium, double in about 25 years. But their demand for British manufactures increases much faster, as the consumption is not merely in proportion to their numbers, but grows with the growing abilities of the same numbers to pay for them. In 1723, the whole importation from Britain to Pennsylvania, was but about 15,000 Pounds Sterling; it is now near Half a Million.

[40] Q. In what light did the people of America use to consider the parliament of Great-Britain?

A. They considered the parliament as the great bulwark and security of their liberties and privileges, and always spoke of it with the utmost respect and veneration. Arbitrary ministers, they thought, might possibly, at times, attempt to oppress them; but they relied on it, that the parliament, on application, would always give redress. They remembered, with gratitude, a strong instance of this, when a bill was brought into parliament, with a clause to make royal instructions laws in the Colonies, which the house of commons would not pass, and it was thrown out.

[41] Q. And have they not still the same respect for parliament?

A. No; it is greatly lessened.

[42] Q. To what causes is that owing?

A. To a concurrence of causes; the restraints lately laid on their trade, by which the bringing of foreign gold and silver into the Colonies was prevented; the prohibition of making paper money among themselves; and then demanding a new and heavy tax by stamps;

Color-Blind Constitution

taking away, at the same time, trials by juries, and refusing to receive and hear their humble petitions.

[43] Q. Don't you think they would submit to the stamp-act, if it was modified, the obnoxious parts taken out, and the duty reduced to some particulars, of small moment?

A. No; they will never submit to it.

[44] Q. What do you think is the reason that the people of America increase faster than in England?

A. Because they marry younger, and more generally.

[45] Q. Why so?

A. Because any young couple that are industrious, may easily obtain land of their own, on which they can raise a family.

[46] Q. Are not the lower rank of people more at their ease in America than in England?

A. They may be so, if they are sober and diligent, as they are better paid for their labour.

[47] Q. What is your opinion of a future tax, imposed on the same principle with that of the stamp-act; how would the Americans receive it?

A. Just as they do this. They would not pay it.

[48] Q. Have you not heard of the resolutions of this house, and of the house of lords, asserting the right of

parliament relating to America, including a power to tax the people there?

A. Yes, I have heard of such resolutions.

[49] Q. What will be the opinion of the Americans on those resolutions?

A. They will think them unconstitutional, and unjust.

[50] Q. Was it an opinion in America before 1763, that the parliament had no right to lay taxes and duties there?

A. I never heard any objection to the right of laying duties to regulate commerce; but a right to lay internal taxes was never supposed to be in parliament, as we are not represented there.

[51] Q. On what do you found your opinion, that the people in America made any such distinction?

A. I know that whenever the subject has occurred in conversation where I have been present, it has appeared to be the opinion of every one, that we could not be taxed in a parliament where we were not represented. But the payment of duties laid by act of parliament, as regulations of commerce, was never disputed.

[52] Q. But can you name any act of assembly, or public act of any of your governments, that made such distinction?

A. I do not know that there was any; I think there was never an occasion to make any such act, till now that you have attempted to tax us; that has occasioned resolutions of assembly, declaring the distinction, in which I think every assembly on the continent, and every member in every assembly, have been unanimous.

[53] Q. What then could occasion conversations on that subject before that time?

A. There was in 1754 a proposition made (I think it came from hence) that in case of a war, which was then apprehended, the governors of the Colonies should meet, and order the levying of troops, building of forts, and taking every other necessary measure for the general defence; and should draw on the treasury here for the sums expended, which were afterwards to be raised in the Colonies by a general tax, to be laid on them by act of parliament. This occasioned a good deal of conversation on the subject, and the general opinion was, that the parliament neither would nor could lay any tax on us, till we were duly represented in parliament, because it was not just, nor agreeable to the nature of an English constitution.

[54] Q. Don't you know there was a time in New-York, when it was under consideration to make an application to parliament to lay taxes on that Colony, upon a deficiency arising from the assembly's refusing or neglecting to raise the necessary supplies for the support of the civil government?

A. I never heard of it.

[55] Q. There was such an application under consideration in New-York; and do you apprehend they could suppose the right of parliament to lay a tax in America was only local, and confined to the case of a deficiency in a particular Colony, by a refusal of its assembly to raise the necessary supplies?

A. They could not suppose such a case, as that the assembly would not raise the necessary supplies to support its own government. An assembly that would refuse it must want common sense, which cannot be supposed. I think there was never any such case at New-York, and that it must be a misrepresentation, or the fact must be misunderstood. I know there have been some attempts, by ministerial instructions from hence, to oblige the assemblies to settle permanent salaries on governors, which they wisely refused to do; but I believe no assembly of New-York, or any other Colony, ever refused duly to support government by proper allowances, from time to time, to public officers.

[56] Q. But in case a governor, acting by instruction, should call on an assembly to raise the necessary supplies, and the assembly should refuse to do it, do you not think it would then be for the good of the people of the colony, as well as necessary to government, that the parliament should tax them?

A. I do not think it would be necessary. If an assembly could possibly be so absurd as to refuse raising the supplies requisite for the maintenance of government among them, they could not long remain in such a situation; the disorders and confusion occasioned by it must soon bring them to reason.

[57] Q. If it should not, ought not the right to be in Great-Britain of applying a remedy?

A. A right only to be used in such a case, I should have no objection to, supposing it to be used merely for the good of the people of the Colony.

[58] Q. But who is to judge of that, Britain or the Colony?

A. Those that feel can best judge.

[59] Q. You say the Colonies have always submitted to external taxes, and object to the right of parliament only in laying internal taxes; now can you shew that there is any kind of difference between the two taxes to the Colony on which they may be laid?

A. I think the difference is very great. An external tax is a duty laid on commodities imported; that duty is added to the first cost, and other charges on the commodity, and when it is offered to sale, makes a part of the price. If the people do not like it at that price, they refuse it; they are not obliged to pay it. But an internal tax is forced from the people without their consent, if not laid by their own representatives. The stamp-act says, we shall have no commerce, make no exchange of property with each other, neither purchase nor grant, nor recover debts; we shall neither marry, nor make our wills, unless we pay such and such sums, and thus it is intended to extort our money from us, or ruin us by the consequences of refusing to pay it.

[60] Q. But supposing the external tax or duty to be laid on the necessaries of life imported into your Colony, will not that be the same thing in its effects as an internal tax?

A. I do not know a single article imported into the Northern Colonies, but what they can either do without, or make themselves.

[61] Q. Don't you think cloth from England absolutely necessary to them?

A. No, by no means absolutely necessary; with industry and good management, they may very well supply themselves with all they want.

[62] Q. Will it not take a long time to establish that manufacture among them? and must they not in the mean while suffer greatly?

A. I think not. They have made a surprising progress already. And I am of opinion, that before their old clothes are worn out, they will have new ones of their own making.

[63] Q. Can they possibly find wool enough in North-America?

A. They have taken steps to increase the wool. They entered into general combinations to eat no more lamb, and very few lambs were killed last year. This course persisted in, will soon make a prodigious difference in the quantity of wool. And the establishing of great manufactories, like those in the clothing towns here, is not necessary, as it is where the business is to be carried on for the purposes of trade. The people will all spin, and work for themselves, in their own houses.

[64] Q. Can there be wool and manufacture enough in one or two years?

A. In three years, I think, there may.

[65] Q. Does not the severity of the winter, in the Northern Colonies, occasion the wool to be of bad quality?

A. No; the wool is very fine and good.

[66] Q. In the more Southern Colonies, as in Virginia; don't you know that the wool is coarse, and only a kind of hair?

A. I don't know it. I never heard it. Yet I have been sometimes in Virginia. I cannot say I ever took particular notice of the wool there, but I believe it is good, though I cannot speak positively of it; but Virginia, and the Colonies south of it, have less occasion for wool; their winters are short, and not very severe, and they can very well clothe themselves with linen and cotton of their own raising for the rest of the year.

[67] Q. Are not the people, in the more Northern Colonies, obliged to fodder their sheep all the winter?

A. In some of the most Northern Colonies they may be obliged to do it some part of the winter.

[68] Q. Considering the resolutions of parliament, as to the right, do you think, if the stamp-act is repealed, that the North Americans will be satisfied?

A. I believe they will.

[69] Q. Why do you think so?

A. I think the resolutions of right will give them very little concern, if they are never attempted to be carried into practice. The Colonies will probably consider themselves in the same situation, in that respect, with Ireland; they know you claim the same right with regard to Ireland, but you never exercise it. And they may believe you never will exercise it in the Colonies, any more than in Ireland, unless on some very extraordinary occasion.

[70] Q. But who are to be the judges of that extraordinary occasion? Is it not the parliament?

A. Though the parliament may judge of the occasion, the people will think it can never exercise such right, till representatives from the Colonies are admitted into parliament, and that whenever the occasion arises, representatives will be ordered.

[71] Q. Did you never hear that Maryland, during the last war, had refused to furnish a quota towards the common defence?

A. Maryland has been much misrepresented in that matter. Maryland, to my knowledge, never refused to contribute, or grant aids to the Crown. The assemblies every year, during the war, voted considerable sums, and formed bills to raise them. The bills were, according to the constitution of that province, sent up to the council, or upper house, for concurrence, that they might be presented to the governor, in order to be enacted into laws. Unhappy disputes between the two houses arising, from the defects of that constitution principally, rendered all the bills but one or two abortive. The proprietary's council rejected them. It is true Maryland did not contribute its proportion, but it was, in my opinion, the fault of the government, not of the people.

[72] Q. Was it not talked of in the other provinces as a proper measure to apply to parliament to compel them?

A. I have heard such discourse; but as it was well known, that the people were not to blame, no such application was ever made, nor any step taken towards it.

[73] Q. Was it not proposed at a public meeting?

A. Not that I know of.

[74] Q. Do you remember the abolishing of the paper currency in New England, by act of assembly?

A. I do remember its being abolished, in the Massachusett's Bay.

[75] Q. Was not Lieutenant Governor Hutchinson principally concerned in that transaction?

A. I have heard so.

[76] Q. Was it not at that time a very unpopular law?

A. I believe it might, though I can say little about it, as I lived at a distance from that province.

[77] Q. Was not the scarcity of gold and silver an argument used against abolishing the paper?

A. I suppose it was.

[78] Q. What is the present opinion there of that law? Is it as unpopular as it was at first?

A. I think it is not.

[79] Q. Have not instructions from hence been sometimes sent over to governors, highly oppressive and unpolitical?

A. Yes.

[80] Q. Have not some governors dispensed with them for that reason?

A. Yes, I have heard so.

[81] Q. Did the Americans ever dispute the controling power of parliament to regulate the commerce?

A. No.

[82] Q. Can any thing less than a military force carry the stamp-act into execution?

A. I do not see how a military force can be applied to that purpose.

[83] Q. Why may it not?

A. Suppose a military force sent into America, they will find nobody in arms; what are they then to do? They cannot force a man to take stamps who chooses to do without them. They will not find a rebellion; they may indeed make one.

[84] Q. If the act is not repealed, what do you think will be the consequences?

A. A total loss of the respect and affection the people of America bear to this country, and of all the commerce that depends on that respect and affection.

[85] Q. How can the commerce be affected?

A. You will find, that if the act is not repealed, they will take very little of your manufactures in a short time.

[86] Q. Is it in their power to do without them?

A. I think they may very well do without them.

[87] Q. Is it their interest not to take them?

A. The goods they take from Britain are either necessaries, mere conveniences, or superfluities. The first, as cloth, &c. with a little industry they can make at home; the second they can do without, till they are able to provide them among themselves; and the last, which are much the greatest part, they will strike off immediately. They are mere articles of fashion, purchased and consumed, because the fashion in a respected country, but will now be detested and rejected.

The people have already struck off, by general agreement, the use of all goods fashionable in mournings, and many thousand pounds worth are sent back as unsaleable.

[88] Q. Is it their interest to make cloth at home?

A. I think they may at present get it cheaper from Britain, I mean of the same fineness and neatness of workmanship; but when one considers other circumstances, the restraints on their trade, and the difficulty of making remittances, it is their interest to make every thing.

[89] Q. Suppose an act of internal regulations, connected with a tax, how would they receive it?

A. I think it would be objected to.

[90] Q. Then no regulation with a tax would be submitted to?

A. Their opinion is, that when aids to the Crown are wanted, they are to be asked of the several assemblies, according to the old established usage, who will, as they always have done, grant them freely. And that their money ought not to be given away without their consent, by persons at a distance, unacquainted with their circumstances and abilities. The granting aids to the Crown, is the only means they have of recommending themselves to their sovereign, and they think it extremely hard and unjust, that a body of men, in which they have no representatives, should make a merit to itself of giving and granting what is not its own, but theirs, and deprive them of a right they esteem of the utmost value and importance, as it is the security of all their other rights.

[91] Q. But is not the post-office, which they have long received, a tax as well as a regulation?

A. No; the money paid for the postage of a letter is not of the nature of a tax; it is merely a quantum meruit for a service done; no person is compellable to pay the money, if he does not chuse to receive the service. A man may still, as before the act, send his letter by a servant, a special messenger, or a friend, if he thinks it cheaper and safer.

[92] Q. But do they not consider the regulations of the postoffice, by the act of last year, as a tax?

A. By the regulations of last year the rate of postage was generally abated near thirty per cent. through all America; they certainly cannot consider such abatement as a tax.

[93] Q. If an excise was laid by parliament, which they might likewise avoid paying, by not consuming the articles excised, would they then not object to it?

A. They would certainly object to it, as an excise is unconnected with any service done, and is merely an aid which they think ought to be asked of them, and granted by them, if they are to pay it, and can be granted for them by no others whatsoever, whom they have not impowered for that purpose.

[94] Q. You say they do not object to the right of parliament in laying duties on goods to be paid on their importation; now, is there any kind of difference between a duty on the importation of goods, and an excise on their consumption?

A. Yes; a very material one; an excise, for the reasons I have just mentioned, they think you can have no right to lay within their country. But the sea is yours; you maintain, by your fleets, the safety of navigation in it; and keep it clear of pirates; you may have therefore a natural and equitable right to some toll or duty on merchandizes carried through that part of your dominions, towards defraying the expence you are at in ships to maintain the safety of that carriage.

[95] Q. Does this reasoning hold in the case of a duty laid on the produce of their lands exported? And would they not then object to such a duty?

A. If it tended to make the produce so much dearer abroad as to lessen the demand for it, to be sure they would object to such a duty; not to your right of laying it, but they would complain of it as a burthen, and petition you to lighten it.

[96] Q. Is not the duty paid on the tobacco exported a duty of that kind?

A. That, I think, is only on tobacco carried coastwise from one Colony to another, and appropriated as a fund for supporting the college at Williamsburgh, in Virginia.

[97] Q. Have not the assemblies in the West-Indies the same natural rights with those in North America?

A. Undoubtedly.

[98] Q. And is there not a tax laid there on their sugars exported?

A. I am not much acquainted with the West-Indies, but the duty of four and a half per cent. on sugars exported, was, I believe, granted by their own assemblies.

[99] Q. How much is the poll-tax in your province laid on unmarried men?

A. It is, I think, Fifteen Shillings, to be paid by every single freeman, upwards of twenty-one years old.

[100] Q. What is the annual amount of all the taxes in Pennsylvania?

A. I suppose about 20,000 Pounds sterling.

[101] Q. Supposing the stamp-act continued, and enforced, do you imagine that ill humour will induce the Americans to give as much for worse manufactures of their own, and use them, preferably to better of ours?

A. Yes, I think so. People will pay as freely to gratify one passion as another, their resentment as their pride.

[102] Q. Would the people at Boston discontinue their trade?

A. The merchants are a very small number, compared with the body of the people, and must discontinue their trade, if nobody will buy their goods.

[103] Q. What are the body of the people in the Colonies?

A. They are farmers, husbandmen or planters.

[104] Q. Would they suffer the produce of their lands to rot?

A. No; but they would not raise so much. They would manufacture more, and plough less.

[105] Q. Would they live without the administration of justice in civil matters, and suffer all the inconveniences of such a situation for any considerable time, rather than take the stamps, supposing the stamps were protected by a sufficient force, where every one might have them?

A. I think the supposition impracticable, that the stamps should be so protected as that every one might have them. The act requires sub-distributors to be appointed in every county town, district and village, and they would be necessary. But the principal distributors, who were to have had a considerable profit on the whole, have not thought it worth while to continue in the office, and I think it impossible to find sub-distributors fit to be trusted, who, for the trifling profit that must come to their share, would incur the odium, and run the hazard that would attend it; and if they could be found, I think it impracticable to protect the stamps in so many distant and remote places.

[106] Q. But in places where they could be protected, would not the people use them rather than remain in such a situation, unable to obtain any right, or recover, by law, any debt?

A. It is hard to say what they would do. I can only judge what other people will think, and how they will act, by what I feel within myself. I have a great many debts due to me in America, and I had rather they should remain unrecoverable by any law, than submit to the stamp-act. They will be debts of honour. It is my opinion the people will either continue in that situation, or find some way to extricate themselves, perhaps by generally agreeing to proceed in the courts without stamps.

[107] Q. What do you think a sufficient military force to protect the distribution of the stamps in every part of America?

A. A very great force; I can't say what, if the disposition of America is for a general resistance.

[108] Q. What is the number of men in America able to bear arms, or of disciplined militia?

A. There are, I suppose, at least—[*Question objected to. He withdrew. Called in again.*]

[109] Q. Is the American stamp-act an equal tax on that country?

A. I think not.

[110] Q. Why so?

A. The greatest part of the money must arise from law suits for the recovery of debts, and be paid by the lower sort of people, who were too poor easily to pay their debts. It is therefore a heavy tax on the poor, and a tax upon them for being poor.

[111] Q. But will not this increase of expence be a means of lessening the number of law suits?

A. I think not; for as the costs all fall upon the debtor, and are to be paid by him, they would be no discouragement to the creditor to bring his action.

[112] Q. Would it not have the effect of excessive usury?

A. Yes, as an oppression of the debtor.

[113] Q. How many ships are there laden annually in North-America with flax-seed for Ireland?

A. I cannot speak to the number of ships, but I know that in 1752, 10,000 hogsheads of flax-seed, each containing 7 bushels, were exported from Philadelphia to Ireland. I suppose the quantity is greatly increased since that time; and it is understood that the exportation from New York is equal to that from Philadelphia.

[114] Q. What becomes of the flax that grows with that flax-seed?

A. They manufacture some into coarse, and some into a middling kind of linen.

[115] Q. Are there any slitting mills in America?

A. I think there are, but I believe only one at present employed. I suppose they will all be set to work, if the interruption of the trade continues.

[116] Q. Are there any fulling mills there?

A. A great many.

[117] Q. Did you never hear that a great quantity of stockings were contracted for for the army, during the war, and manufactured in Philadelphia?

A. I have heard so.

[118] Q. If the stamp act should be repealed, would not the Americans think they could oblige the parliament to repeal every external tax law now in force?

A. It is hard to answer questions of what people at such a distance will think.

[119] Q. But what do you imagine they will think were the motives of repealing the act?

A. I suppose they will think that it was repealed from a conviction of its inexpediency; and they will rely upon it, that while the same inexpediency subsists, you will never attempt to make such another.

[120] Q. What do you mean by its inexpediency?

A. I mean its inexpediency on several accounts; the poverty and inability of those who were to pay the tax;

the general discontent it has occasioned; and the impracticability of enforcing it.

[121] Q. If the act should be repealed, and the legislature should shew its resentment to the opposers of the stamp-act, would the Colonies acquiesce in the authority of the legislature? What is your opinion they would do?

A. I don't doubt at all, that if the legislature repeal the stamp-act, the Colonies will acquiesce in the authority.

[122] Q. But if the legislature should think fit to ascertain its right to lay taxes, by any act laying a small tax, contrary to their opinion, would they submit to pay the tax?

A. The proceedings of the people in America have been considered too much together. The proceedings of the assemblies have been very different from those of the mobs, and should be distinguished, as having no connection with each other. The assemblies have only peaceably resolved what they take to be their rights; they have taken no measures for opposition by force; they have not built a fort, raised a man, or provided a grain of ammunition, in order to such opposition. The ringleaders of riots they think ought to be punished; they would punish them themselves, if they could. Every sober sensible man would wish to see rioters punished; as otherwise peaceable people have no security of person or estate. But as to any internal tax, how small soever, laid by the legislature here on the people there, while they have no representatives in this legislature, I think it will never be submitted to. They will oppose it to the last. They do not consider it as at all necessary for you to raise money on them by your taxes, because they are, and always have been, ready to raise money by taxes among themselves, and to grant large sums, equal to their abilities, upon requisition from the Crown. They have not only granted equal to their abilities, but, during all the last war, they granted far beyond their abilities, and beyond their proportion with this country, you yourselves being judges, to the amount of many hundred thousand pounds, and this they did freely and readily, only on a sort of promise from the secretary of state, that it should be recommended to parliament to make them compensation. It was accordingly recommended to parliament, in the most honourable manner, for them. America has been greatly misrepresented and abused here, in papers, and pamphlets, and speeches, as ungrateful, and unreasonable, and unjust, in having put this nation to immense expence for their defence, and refusing to bear any part of that expence. The Colonies raised, paid and clothed, near 25000 men during the last war, a number equal to those sent from Britain, and far beyond their proportion; they went deeply into debt in doing this, and all their taxes and estates are mortgaged, for many years to come, for discharging that debt. Government here was at that time very sensible of this. The Colonies were recommended to parliament. Every year the King sent down to the house a written message to this purpose, That his Majesty, being highly sensible of the zeal and vigour with which his faithful subjects in

North-America had exerted themselves, in defence of his Majesty's just rights and possessions, recommended it to the house to take the same into consideration, and enable him to give them a proper compensation. You will find those messages on your own journals every year of the war to the very last, and you did accordingly give 200,000 Pounds annually to the Crown, to be distributed in such compensation to the Colonies. This is the strongest of all proofs that the Colonies, far from being unwilling to bear a share of the burthen, did exceed their proportion; for if they had done less, or had only equalled their proportion, there would have been no room or reason for compensation. Indeed the sums reimbursed them, were by no means adequate to the expence they incurred beyond their proportion; but they never murmured at that; they esteemed their Sovereign's approbation of their zeal and fidelity, and the approbation of this house, far beyond any other kind of compensation; therefore there was no occasion for this act, to force money from a willing people; they had not refused giving money for the purposes of the act; no requisition had been made; they were always willing and ready to do what could reasonably be expected from them, and in this light they wish to be considered.

[123] Q. But suppose Great-Britain should be engaged in a war in Europe, would North-America contribute to the support of it?

A. I do think they would, as far as their circumstances would permit. They consider themselves as a part of the British empire, and as having one common interest with it; they may be looked on here as foreigners, but they do not consider themselves as such. They are zealous for the honour and prosperity of this nation, and, while they are well used, will always be ready to support it, as far as their little power goes. In 1739 they were called upon to assist in the expedition against Carthagena, and they sent 3000 men to join your army. It is true Carthagena is in America, but as remote from the Northern Colonies, as if it had been in Europe. They make no distinction of wars, as to their duty of assisting in them. I know the last war is commonly spoke of here as entered into for the defence, or for the sake of the people of America. I think it is quite misunderstood. It began about the limits between Canada and Nova-Scotia, about territories to which the Crown indeed laid claim, but were not claimed by any British Colony; none of the lands had been granted to any Colonist; we had therefore no particular concern or interest in that dispute. As to the Ohio, the contest there began about your right of trading in the Indian country, a right you had by the treaty of Utrecht, which the French infringed; they seized the traders and their goods, which were your manufactures; they took a fort which a company of your merchants, and their factors and correspondents, had erected there, to secure that trade. Braddock was sent with an army to re-take that fort (which was looked on here as another incroachment on the King's territory) and to protect your trade. It was not till after his defeat that the Colonies were attacked. They were before in perfect peace with both French and Indians; the troops were not therefore sent for their defence. The trade with the

Indians, though carried on in America, is not an American interest. The people of America are chiefly farmers and planters; scarce any thing that they raise or produce is an article of commerce with the Indians. The Indian trade is a British interest; it is carried on with British manufactures, for the profit of British merchants and manufacturers; therefore the war, as it commenced for the defence of territories of the Crown, the property of no American, and for the defence of a trade purely British, was really a British war—and yet the people of America made no scruple of contributing their utmost towards carrying it on, and bringing it to a happy conclusion.

[124] Q. Do you think then that the taking possession of the King's territorial rights, and strengthening the frontiers, is not an American interest?

A. Not particularly, but conjointly a British and an American interest.

[125] Q. You will not deny that the preceding war, the war with Spain, was entered into for the sake of America; was it not occasioned by captures made in the American seas?

A. Yes; captures of ships carrying on the British trade there, with British manufactures.

[126] Q. Was not the late war with the Indians, since the peace with France, a war for America only?

A. Yes; it was more particularly for America than the former, but it was rather a consequence or remains of the former war, the Indians not having been thoroughly pacified, and the Americans bore by much the greatest share of the expence. It was put an end to by the army under General Bouquet; there were not above 300 regulars in that army, and above 1000 Pennsylvanians.

[127] Q. Is it not necessary to send troops to America, to defend the Americans against the Indians?

A. No, by no means; it never was necessary. They defended themselves when they were but an handful, and the Indians much more numerous. They continually gained ground, and have driven the Indians over the mountains, without any troops sent to their assistance from this country. And can it be thought necessary now to send troops for their defence from those diminished Indian tribes, when the Colonies are become so populous, and so strong? There is not the least occasion for it; they are very able to defend themselves.

[128] Q. Do you say there were no more than 300 regular troops employed in the late Indian war?

A. Not on the Ohio, or the frontiers of Pennsylvania, which was the chief part of the war that affected the Colonies. There were garrisons at Niagara, Fort Detroit, and those remote posts kept for the sake of your trade; I did not reckon them, but I believe that on the whole the number of Americans, or provincial troops, employed in the war, was greater than that of the regulars. I am not certain, but I think so.

[129] Q. Do you think the assemblies have a right to levy money on the subject there, to grant to the Crown?

A. I certainly think so; they have always done it.

[130] Q. Are they acquainted with the declaration of rights? And do they know that, by that statute, money is not to be raised on the subject but by consent of parliament?

A. They are very well acquainted with it.

[131] Q. How then can they think they have a right to levy money for the Crown, or for any other than local purposes?

A. They understand that clause to relate to subjects only within the realm; that no money can be levied on them for the Crown, but by consent of parliament. The Colonies are not supposed to be within the realm; they have assemblies of their own, which are their parliaments, and they are in that respect, in the same situation with Ireland. When money is to be raised for the Crown upon the subject in Ireland, or in the Colonies, the consent is given in the parliament of Ireland, or in the assemblies of the Colonies. They think the parliament of Great-Britain cannot properly give that consent till it has representatives from America; for the petition of right expressly says, it is to be by common consent in parliament, and the people of America have no representatives in parliament, to make a part of that common consent.

[132] Q. If the stamp-act should be repealed, and an act should pass, ordering the assemblies of the Colonies to indemnify the sufferers by the riots, would they obey it?

A. That is a question I cannot answer.

[133] Q. Suppose the King should require the Colonies to grant a revenue, and the parliament should be against their doing it, do they think they can grant a revenue to the King, without the consent of the parliament of G. Britain?

A. That is a deep question. As to my own opinion, I should think myself at liberty to do it, and should do it, if I liked the occasion.

[134] Q. When money has been raised in the Colonies, upon requisitions, has it not been granted to the King?

A. Yes, always; but the requisitions have generally been for some service expressed, as to raise, clothe and pay troops, and not for money only.

[135] Q. If the act should pass, requiring the American assemblies to make compensation to the sufferers, and they should disobey it, and then the parliament should, by another act, lay an internal tax, would they then obey it?

A. The people will pay no internal tax; and I think an act to oblige the assemblies to make compensation is unnecessary, for I am of opinion, that as soon as the present heats are abated, they will take the matter into consideration, and, if it is right to be done, they will do it of themselves.

[136] Q. Do not letters often come into the post-offices in America, directed to some inland town where no post goes?

A. Yes.

[137] Q. Can any private person take up those letters, and carry them as directed?

A. Yes; any friend of the person may do it, paying the postage that has occurred.

[138] Q. But must he not pay an additional postage for the distance to such inland town?

A. No.

[139] Q. Can the post-master answer delivering the letter, without being paid such additional postage?

A. Certainly he can demand nothing, where he does no service.

[140] Q. Suppose a person, being far from home, finds a letter in a post-office directed to him, and he lives in a place to which the post generally goes, and the letter is directed to that place, will the post-master deliver him the letter, without his paying the postage receivable at the place to which the letter is directed?

A. Yes; the office cannot demand postage for a letter that it does not carry, or farther than it does carry it.

[141] Q. Are not ferrymen in America obliged, by act of parliament, to carry over the posts without pay?

A. Yes.

[142] Q. Is not this a tax on the ferrymen?

A. They do not consider it as such, as they have an advantage from persons travelling with the post.

[143] Q. If the stamp-act should be repealed, and the Crown should make a requisition to the Colonies for a sum of money, would they grant it?

A. I believe they would.

[144] Q. Why do you think so?

A. I can speak for the Colony I live in; I had it in instruction from the assembly to assure the ministry, that as they always had done, so they should always think it their duty to grant such aids to the Crown as were suitable to their circumstances and abilities, whenever called upon for the purpose, in the usual constitutional manner; and I had the honour of communicating this instruction to that honourable gentleman then minister.

[145] Q. Would they do this for a British concern; as suppose a war in some part of Europe, that did not affect them?

A. Yes, for any thing that concerned the general interest. They consider themselves as a part of the whole.

[146] Q. What is the usual constitutional manner of calling on the Colonies for aids?

A. A letter from the secretary of state.

[147] Q. Is this all you mean, a letter from the secretary of state?

A. I mean the usual way of requisition, in a circular letter from the secretary of state, by his Majesty's command, reciting the occasion, and recommending it to the Colonies to grant such aids as became their loyalty, and were suitable to their abilities.

[148] Q. Did the secretary of state ever write for money for the Crown?

A. The requisitions have been to raise, clothe and pay men, which cannot be done without money.

[149] Q. Would they grant money alone, if called on?

A. In my opinion they would, money as well as men, when they have money, or can make it.

[150] Q. If the parliament should repeal the stamp-act, will the assembly of Pennsylvania rescind their resolutions?

A. I think not.

[151] Q. Before there was any thought of the stamp-act, did they wish for a representation in parliament?

A. No.

[152 Q. Don't you know that there is, in the Pennsylvania charter, an express reservation of the right of parliament to lay taxes there?

A. I know there is a clause in the charter, by which the King grants that he will levy no taxes on the inhabitants, unless it be with the consent of the assembly, or by act of parliament.

[153] Q. How then could the assembly of Pennsylvania assert, that laying a tax on them by the stamp-act was an infringement of their rights?

A. They understand it thus; by the same charter, and otherwise, they are intitled to all the privileges and liberties of Englishmen; they find in the great charters, and the petition and declaration of rights, that one of the privileges of English subjects is, that they are not to be taxed but by their common consent; they have therefore relied upon it, from the first settlement of the province, that the parliament never would, nor could, by colour of that clause in the charter, assume a right of taxing them, till it had qualified itself to exercise such right, by admitting representatives from the people to be taxed, who ought to make a part of that common consent.

[154] Q. Are there any words in the charter that justify that construction?

A. The common rights of Englishmen, as declared by Magna Charta, and the petition of right, all justify it.

[155] Q. Does the distinction between internal and external taxes exist in the words of the charter?

A. No, I believe not.

[156] Q. Then may they not, by the same interpretation, object to the parliament's right of external taxation?

A. They never have hitherto. Many arguments have been lately used here to shew them that there is no difference, and that if you have no right to tax them internally, you have none to tax them externally, or make any other law to bind them. At present they do not reason so, but in time they may possibly be convinced by these arguments.

[157] Q. Do not the resolutions of the Pennsylvania assembly say all taxes?

A. If they do, they mean only internal taxes; the same words have not always the same meaning here and in the Colonies. By taxes they mean internal taxes; by duties they mean customs; these are their ideas of the language.

[158] Q. Have you not seen the resolutions of the Massachusett's Bay assembly?

A. I have.

[159] Q. Do they not say, that neither external nor internal taxes can be laid on them by parliament?

A. I don't know that they do; I believe not.

[160] Q. If the same Colony should say neither tax nor imposition could be laid, does not that province hold the power of parliament can hold neither?[3]

A. I suppose that by the word imposition, they do not intend to express duties to be laid on goods imported, as regulations of commerce.

[161] Q. What can the Colonies mean then by imposition as distinct from taxes?

A. They may mean many things, as impressing of men, or of carriages, quartering troops on private houses, and the like; there may be great impositions, that are not properly taxes.

[162] Q. Is not the post-office rate an internal tax laid by act of parliament?

A. I have answered that.

[163] Q. Are all parts of the Colonies equally able to pay taxes?

A. No, certainly; the frontier parts, which have been ravaged by the enemy, are greatly disabled by that means, and therefore, in such cases, are usually favoured in our tax-laws.

[164] Q. Can we, at this distance, be competent judges of what favours are necessary?

A. The Parliament have supposed it, by claiming a right to make tax laws for America; I think it impossible.

[165] Q. Would the repeal of the stamp-act be any discouragement of your manufactures? Will the people that have begun to manufacture decline it?

A. Yes, I think they will; especially if, at the same time, the trade is opened again, so that remittances can be easily made. I have known several instances that make it probable. In the war before last, tobacco being low, and making little remittance, the people of Virginia went generally into family manufactures. Afterwards, when tobacco bore a better price, they returned to the use of British manufactures. So fulling mills were very much disused in the last war in Pennsylvania, because bills were then plenty, and remittances could easily be made to Britain for English cloth and other goods.

[166] Q. If the stamp-act should be repealed, would it induce the assemblies of America to acknowledge the rights of parliament to tax them, and would they erase their resolutions?

A. No, never.

[167] Q. Is there no means of obliging them to erase those resolutions?

A. None that I know of; they will never do it unless compelled by force of arms.

[168] Q. Is there a power on earth that can force them to erase them?

A. No power, how great soever, can force men to change their opinions.

[169] Q. Do they consider the post-office as a tax, or as a regulation?

A. Not as a tax, but as a regulation and conveniency; every assembly encouraged it, and supported it in its infancy, by grants of money, which they would not otherwise have done; and the people have always paid the postage.

[170] Q. When did you receive the instructions you mentioned?

A. I brought them with me, when I came to England, about 15 months since.

[171] Q. When did you communicate that instruction to the minister?

A. Soon after my arrival, while the stamping of America was under consideration, and before the bill was brought in.

[172] Q. Would it be most for the interest of Great-Britain, to employ the hands of Virginia in tobacco, or in manufactures?

A. In tobacco to be sure.

[173] Q. What used to be the pride of the Americans?

A. To indulge in the fashions and manufactures of Great-Britain.

[174] Q. What is now their pride?

A. To wear their old cloaths over again, till they can make new ones.

Withdrew——The end.

Soon, upon the close of Dr. Franklin's testimony—the question of repealing the *Stamp Act* was taken under advisement for a solemn disposition by Parliament's House of Commons.

The imperial government recognized that it looked like it was debating and repealing the *Stamp Act* due to the British government's waning control over the American colonies. Yet, issues concerning repealing the *Stamp Act* were undeniably inextricably interwoven with parliamentary reform. Moreover, while Great Britain was technically ruled by parliament, the British Parliament bore only marginal relation to a representative assembly. By the reign of King George III, there had been no redistribution of parliamentary "representation" for over two centuries. Thus, the fundamental problem was the abandonment of salutary neglect regarding the American colonies in 1763; it required a reconciliation of centralized imperial control concerning colonial home rule, which Parliament had not considered or done.

The majority of the members of Parliament did not like the perception of relenting toward the American colonies and resisted repealing the *Stamp Act*. Ultimately, both houses of Parliament voted for repealing and enacting the *Declaratory Act* on March 18, 1766. Since the two bills were passed together, they became known as the *"Twin Brothers"* and were connected. Thus, Parliament addressed Dr. Franklin's legal arguments in the *Declaratory Act* to the chagrin of the southern colonial elite and its legislators.

The Declaratory Act: March 18, 1766

An act for the better securing the dependency of his majesty's dominions in America upon the crown and parliament of Great Britain.

Whereas several of the houses of representatives in His Majesty's colonies and plantations in America have, of late, against the law, claimed to themselves, or to the general assemblies of the same, the sole and exclusive right of imposing duties and taxes upon his majesty's subjects in the said colonies and plantations; and have in pursuance of such claim, passed certain votes, resolutions, and orders derogatory to the legislative authority of parliament, and inconsistent with the dependency Of the said colonies and plantations upon the crown of Great Britain; may it therefore please your most excellent Majesty, that it may be declared; and be it declared by the Kinbg's most excellent majesty, by and with the advice and consent of the lords spiritual and temporal, and commons, in this present parliament assembled, and by the authority of the same, That the said colonies and plantations in America have been, are, and of right ought to be, subordinate unto, and dependent upon the imperial crown and parliament of Great Britain; and that the King's majesty, by and with the advice and consent of the lords spiritual and temporal and commons of Great Britain, in parliament assembled, had, bath, and of right ought to have, full power and authority to make laws and statutes of sufficient force and validity to bind the colonies and people of America, subjects of the crown of Great Britain, in all cases whatsoever.

The Declaratory Act of 1766; Section II provided:

II. AND BE IT FURTHER DECLARED and enacted by authority aforesaid, That all resolutions, votes, orders, and proceedings, in any of the said colonies or plantations, whereby the power and authority of the parliament of GREAT BRITAIN, to make laws and statutes as aforesaid, is denied, or drawn into question, are, and are hereby declared to be, utterly null and void to all intents and purposes whatsoever.

The *Declaratory Act of 1766* was self-executing,[33] and the political reasonings on the part of the imperial government to not enforce the law—good, evil, or corrupt and/or the possible misapprehension of this law within the American colonies had no legal consequence or effect upon the legality of the *Declaratory Act of 1766*, nor did it forestall its legal effect upon colonial America or the colonial Englishmen living within the American colonies.

Under the English rule of law, an act of Parliament is presumptively controlling law in the realm, making it the law of the land, [34] as the Parliament was the supreme legislative authority in the Kingdom of Great Britain during colonial times. [35] Moreover, the plain language in this English legislation reveals that Parliament did indeed nullify all colonial hereditary slave legislation since such chattel slave practices and customs in colonial America "denied" and did call into question Parliament's power and authority to legislate within the American colonies—as a matter of the English rule of law.

Further, one needs only consider Britain's overarching rationale for enacting the *Declaratory Act of 1766*—which were the *Declaration of Rights and Grievances* and Dr. Benjamin Franklin's two legal arguments attacking parliamentary sovereignty: (1) the Americans believed that Parliament had no legal right to tax them, and (2) that Parliament had no legal authority whatsoever to make any law of any kind regarding the colonies. Both legal arguments were rejected as Parliament declared that it had "full power and authority to make laws and statutes of sufficient force and validity to bind the colonies and people of America, subjects of the crown of Great Britain in all cases whatsoever" and abolished "all resolutions, votes, orders, and proceedings, in any of the said colonies or plantations, whereby the power and authority of Great Britain, to make laws and statutes as aforesaid, is denied or drawn into question, are, and are hereby declared to be utterly null and void to all intents and purposes whatsoever."

In his book *The Majority of the People*, the political theorist Edwin Mims made the statement that "when in 1766 this modernized British Parliament, committed by now to the principle of parliamentary sovereignty unlimited and unlimitable, issued a declaration that a parliamentary majority could pass any law it saw fit, it was greeted with an outcry of horror in the colonies."

Northern patriot leaders such as John Adams, Samuel Adams, and John Dickinson saw trouble coming. Dickinson criticized Parliament in a newspaper for clamping down on colonists' rights while calling upon his countrymen to resist. [36] Dickinson, in presuming that colonial assemblies had correctly and legally enacted all colonial resolutions, votes, orders, and proceedings throughout the American colonies, marginalized the Act outright, writing "instantly on repealing the stamp-act, an act passed, declaring the power of parliament to bind these colonies in all cases whatsoever. This, however, was only planting a barren tree that cast a shade in dread over the colonies but yielded no fruit."

Dickinson also believed the *Declaratory Act* was purposefully ambiguous and designed to hide Parliament's true intentions. Moreover, as the Act was celebrated in the colonies, the Americans thought Parliament had sided with them—when, in reality, it allowed Parliament to reclaim unprecedented authority, which it had, in effect, relinquished during the period of salutary neglect to make any and all laws concerning the American colonies.

This is understandable since many members of Parliament were reluctant to repeal the *Stamp Act* as they thought it would make Britain look weak and would send the message that all people had to do was protest and riot against Parliament, and they would back down to their demands. The remedy was the *Declaratory Act*, which stated that Parliament had "full power and authority to make laws and statutes of sufficient force and validity to bind the colonies and people of America, subjects of the crown of Great Britain, in all cases whatsoever," which is significant as the two houses of Parliament were not unanimous on the *Declaratory Act of 1766*.

This conclusion is consistent with the reporting that an American shared with his friend in Massachusetts. He stated that it was reassuring "to hear that the great PITT, Mr. BARRE, and two or three others" opposed the Act in the House of Commons, and some "opposed also the first resolve in the House of Lords, but a resolve of the right of taxation made." [37] Before the Parliament, William Pitt made a speech defending the Americans, asserting it was his "opinion that this Kingdom has no right to lay a tax upon the colonies." However, Pitt also acknowledged the King's "authority in all things, with the sole exception that you shall not take their money out of their pockets without their consent," but plainly stated also that Parliament was "sovereign and supreme, in every circumstance of government and legislature whatsoever."

In this context, Parliament's repealing and then passing the *Declaratory Act* is consistent with the writing of that American in London who wrote, "There are many, in both houses... who are vehemently against giving way in the least—but would force an implicit obedience even with fire and sword, if necessary—but thank God a great majority are for softer measures." [38]

This letter from this American in London, its publication in multiple colonial newspapers, and other historical also support the conclusion that the repealing of the *Stamp Act* and the passing of the *Declaratory Act* in tandem was not a unified Parliamentary effort—but was discussed by the members and even disputed by prominent Whig leader Willliam Pitt. Thus, American allies in London and their supporters in Parliament probably advised the Americans that there would be no enforcement of section II of the *Declaratory Act* by the imperial government—which occurred.

Moreover, it is significant—that some present-day historians do recognize that the *Declaratory Act* was indeed a reaffirmation of the imperial government's abandonment of salutary neglect and that it was an expression of imperial power which also caused Lord Rockingham's early resignation and the abolishment of all colonial legislation enacted by colonial assemblies within the American colonies "utterly null and void," which "denied" or "questioned" parliamentary laws in 1766. Thus, colonial legislative fiats, hereditary slave legislation, and slave laws throughout the American colonies as they "denied" and "questioned" Parliament's power and authority became null and void under the Act.

Further, many scholars have long believed Dr. Benjamin Franklin's frank discussion with Parliament opened the eyes of many members to realize they were not going to win the fight over the *Stamp Act*. However, perhaps a better view and characterization of Dr. Franklin's examination is Parliament's realization after hearing Dr. Franklin's thoughts was that it gave Parliament greater focus and a better understanding of the more significant threat to the continued British imperial governance within the American colonies: colonial resolutions, votes, orders, and proceedings passed by inferior legislative bodies during the period of salutary neglect denying and drawing into question parliamentary sovereignty.

Many Americans sided with Parliament, such as H. S. Conway, who wrote a letter to Governor Bernard of Massachusetts in June 1766 describing Parliament's *Declaratory Act*. He stated: "The Moderation, the Forbearance, the unexplained Lenity and Tenderness of Parliament towards the Colonies... cannot but dispose the Province committed to your Case, to that Return of cheerful Obedience to the Laws and Legislative Authority of Great Britain." [39] Conway believed the Parliament had bent over backward for the colonists by holding no ill will towards them after the riots spurred by the *Stamp Act*. He argued that the least the colonists could do was to be obedient to Great Britain's legislative authority.

Overshadowed by the dramatic repeal of the *Stamp Act,* which had caused riots and civil unrest in colonial America, the passage of the *Declaratory Act* was given little attention by colonials in 1766. However, the *Declaratory Act of 1766* was an expression of British imperial politics directed at the American colonies and in recalibrated colonial governance. It reaffirmed its abandonment of salutary neglect by stating it had "full power and authority to make laws and statutes of sufficient force and validity to bind the colonies and people of America, subjects of the crown of Great Britain, in all cases whatsoever." The Act stated that "all resolutions, votes, orders, and proceedings" in the American colonies that denied or questioned Parliament's power and authority to make laws binding the colonies "in all cases whatsoever" were "utterly null and void." Thus, the *Declaratory Act* responded to Dr. Benjamin Franklin's testimony but rejected his core representations, which he made on February 13, 1766, before Parliament's House of Commons.

Under the Anglo-Saxon jurisprudential doctrine of parliamentary sovereignty—the Parliament of Great Britain could make legislation on any subject it wished during colonial times. There were no legal limits on Parliament's law-making powers,[40] and the *Declaratory Act of 1766* abolished all colonial resolutions, votes, orders, and proceedings that either denied or questioned its law-making power and authority. Hereditary slavery resolutions and slave laws passed by colonial assemblies in America became utterly null and void" since they violated parliamentary laws. Under the English rule of law, once Parliament enacted a law—it automatically became the law of the land, and it is irrelevant that colonial Americans misinterpreted the Act.

Many historians argue that the *Declaratory Act of 1766* wording was vague enough to allow people of different constitutional persuasions to read into it what they wanted. For example, the act could be seen as including or excluding the authority to tax—mainly if one adhered to the notion that there was a difference between legislation and taxation. However, the question of inclusion or exclusion of taxing authority is not the issue. Instead, Parliament's purposeful wording in section II of the *Declaratory Act* is at issue, where it stated "all resolutions, votes, orders and proceedings" in the American colonies where "the power and authority of the parliament of Great Britain, to make laws and statutes" ... "is denied or drawn into question, are, and are, hereby declared to be, utterly null and void to all intents and purposes whatsoever."

Presumptively, historians, scholars, and others might continue to suggest that the *Declaratory Act* was a mere warning proffered by Parliament to the American colonies in the aftermath of being forced to repeal the *Stamp Act* or that this act did not abolish any resolutions, votes, orders, or proceedings since none of the colonial assemblies had ever dared to declare that Parliament had no legislative authority and power over the American colonies. This is untrue, as the *Declaratory Act of 1766* was a performative expression of imperial governmental power, and to see it differently requires ignoring the imperial government's motivation and the transatlantic tensions created by its enactment of the *Stamp Act* and the imperial government's abandonment of the unofficial policy of salutary neglect toward the American colonies in 1763. The plain meaning and understanding of the words in the act is unambiguous.

During salutary neglect, the imperial government avoided the strict enforcement of parliamentary laws within the American colonies as long as the colonies remained loyal to the government and contributed to the imperial government. Primarily, what ended salutary neglect in 1763 was the end of the *Seven Years' War* against France, in which Britain had gained a vast amount of new territory in North America and debts. [41]

Historians became satisfied after researching each colonial assembly's legislative history when they found no instances where a colonial American resolution, vote, order, or proceeding "denied" Parliament's power and authority to make laws and statutes. This was a mistaken approach, as the legislative historical research should have also sought out "all [colonial] resolutions, votes, orders, and proceedings" that ran afoul of or contradicted established parliamentary laws such as the *Royal Assent by Commission Act of 1541* and *Sedition Act of 1661*.

Denying Parliament's power and authority is distinctly different than "questioning" Parliament's power and authority to make laws—such as what occurs when a colonial assembly ignores or violates a law or statute enacted by Parliament, such as the *English Bill of Rights of 1689* and Virginia's enacting *Slave Laws of 1705*. Thus, whether a product of ignorance—tardiness—the conjunctive structure of the act or the wording in the act itself, the burden was on the colonial lawmakers, elites, and enslavers to secure competent legal counsel or to bring litigation in the colonial courts. Having failed to do any of these actions, revisionist historians cannot be heard complaining.

Moreover, the English doctrine "no man is above the law, and no man is below it, nor do we ask man's permission when we ask him to obey it. Obedience to the law is demanded as a right, not asked as a favor" was the cornerstone of Anglo-Saxon jurisprudence during colonial times. Along with the doctrine, "ignorance of the law is no defense."

Courts have frequently referred to parliamentary sovereignty as a critical principle of the British constitution.[42] Parliament's act in 1766 recalibrated the imperial government's relationship with the American colonies by abolishing "all resolutions, votes, orders, and proceedings" passed by its colonial assemblies that "denied" or "questioned" the power and authority of Parliament by declaring them "utterly null and void" on March 18, 1766. .

In exercising Parliamentary sovereignty, the imperial government rendered all colonial fiats based upon the colonial resolution of *partus sequitur ventrem* "utterly null and void" since they violated parliamentary law, in particular, the *Sedition Act of 1661,* which made it a criminal offense to purport to enact a law without securing the King's assent and, in the absence of the imperial government's assent, were legal nullities. It returned black colonials enslaved at birth due to colonial tyranny to the status *quo ante* in March 1766—ten years before the Declaration of Independence.

The Kingdom of Great Britain during the 1760s had a predominantly political as opposed to a predominantly legal constitution—as any limits on the Parliament's power to enact legislation came from political pressure—not from the law. Thus, as the Kingdom did not have a written constitution, taxing colonial subjects without representation in Parliament was constitutional. Parliamentary sovereignty, as applied during the 1760s concerning the American colonies, did not provide for entrenchment. If it had—such would have destroyed parliamentary sovereignty in the Kingdom—which did not occur.

British Prime Minister George Grenville proposed additional taxes—the *Sugar Act* in 1764, the *Currency Act* in 1765, and the *Stamp Act* also in 1765— all aimed to increase Parliament's authority and revenue from the American colonies. These were unpopular in the colonies, leading to the *Stamp Act* riots in August 1765 and Grenville's resignation. [43] Grenville's successor, Lord Rockingham, asked Dr. Benjamin Franklin to appear before the House of Commons. He agreed, and it was Parliament's frank discussion with Franklin on February 13, 1766—during its deliberation to repeal the *Stamp Act,* which enlightened that supreme legislative body and gave Parliament its principal reasoning for passing the *Declaratory Act of 1766* on March 18, 1766.

For his part, Dr. Franklin's testimony revealed that the American colonial assemblies did not subscribe to the doctrine of parliamentary sovereignty and that the Americans believed Parliament had no legal right to tax them. Moreover, Franklin claimed Parliament had no legal authority whatsoever to make any laws within the colonies. Parliament was incredulous, incensed, and rejected both legal arguments.

Further, Parliament was mindful that under each colonial charter—colonial assemblies were only one house in each colonial legislature—along with England's King, and colonial assemblies were never granted authority and power to enact a positive law in their respective colony. Furthermore, Parliament was well aware that it passed the *Sedition Act in 1661,* which criminalized the utterance of pretended legislation by inferior legislative assemblies without the assent of England's King.

Significantly, in the *Declaratory Act*, Parliament declared "all resolutions, votes, orders, and proceedings" which either denied or "drawn into question," Parliament's power and authority to make laws were declared "null and void." Parliament understood that any resolution passed by a colonial assembly that overrode or conflicted with parliamentary law had drawn into question the power and authority of Parliament as a matter of law. Further, colonial assemblies knew that their hereditary slave resolutions and slave laws were all repugnant to parliamentary laws.

Given the plain language in the act, everyone recognized that a challenge to Parliament exercising parliamentary sovereignty over the American colonies, abolishing its hereditary slave resolutions, votes, orders, and proceedings that denied or questioned Parliament's authority and power would be a futile and wasteful exercise. Stated plainly, the *Declaratory Act of 1766* reaffirmed the end of salutary neglect within the American colonies, which concluded in 1763. Dr. Franklin's examination before Parliament in February 1766 affirmed that this law was needed.

Secondly, Parliament had the right to make and unmake laws within the Kingdom as it saw fit. Nothing prevented Parliament from abolishing previous laws enacted by the colonial American assemblies during salutary neglect for good or no reason. Moreover, there was never a legal requirement for colonial America's governments to have done what the act outlawed, to respond to the *Declaratory Act of 1766,* or for colonial Americans to oppose its enactment to confer legitimacy to this act. In England, Parliament historically did not enact a comprehensive code of legislation. It was left to the courts to develop.[44] Once an interpretation of Parliament's legislation was decided—the court's decision would become binding upon subsequent courts. However, the statutory construction of the *Declaratory Act of 1766* was never questioned or litigated for various reasons.

Additionally, in the context of statutory interpretation—a tribunal is bound to apply the plain language of a statute. If the language is unambiguous, the tribunal should commonly interpret and use it. Further, even if no court decision ever interpreted section II of the *Declaratory Act*, all putative colonial legislation was jurisdictionally defective since Parliament was the only legislature empowered to enact a "positive law" within the Kingdom of Great Britain and the *Somerset* decision in 1772 ruled slavery could only be a lawful condition by way of a "positive law."

According to the Court of the King's Bench in the *Somerset* case in 1772, colonial slave statutes and laws were ineffectual and failed to create a state and condition of slavery. As Parliament had not exercised its supreme legislative authority and power to do so, slavery was disallowed and disapproved by the laws of the Kingdom of Great Britain. Such colonial hereditary slave statutes and slave laws were void ab *initio* for want of jurisdiction. [45] Thus, as a matter of the English rule of law—all of the colonial legislation within the American colonies that did not have the assent of England's King, as well as those that "denied" or "questioned" the personal liberty rights of black colonials granted by Parliament were rendered "null and void" based upon section II of the *Declaratory Act of 1766.*

Each colonial charter required its colonial assembly to secure the assent of the King on any proposed colonial legislative proceedings or enactments. Further, colonial assemblies were obligated to adhere to the English rule of law, and since—all colonial legislation enacted without the assent of England's King violated Parliament's *Royal Assent by Commission Act of 1541* and the *Sedition Act of 1661,* they were void *ab initio,* as well as all "resolutions, votes, orders, and proceedings" that "denied" or "questioned" personal liberty rights of black colonials which the Parliament had conferred unto all Englishmen with its enactment of the *English Bill of Rights of 1689* became "utterly null and void" to "all intents and purposes whatsoever." Thus, black colonials had the same legal status as white colonials when the patriots declared the thirteen colonies' independence from Great Britain in July 1776, as ignorance of the law was no defense.

Parliament's enactment of the *Royal Assent by Commission Act of 1541* made the formal assent of the English King a legal requirement to enact a statute or a law within the Kingdom of Great Britain. It follows in the absence of the King's assent, a legislative action cannot be deemed a law. Subsequently, Parliament's *Sedition Act of 1661* criminalized the errant enactment or "suggestion" of putative legislation within the Kingdom without the King's assent. A careful review of colonial slave legislation would reveal that none of the colonial assemblies within the American colonies ever secured the King's assent regarding the practice of hereditary slavery. Thus, as a matter of English law— all such legislative proceedings in colonial America without the assent of England's King "denied" or otherwise "questioned" the "power and authority of Parliament to make laws and statutes" since Parliament enacted the *Royal Assent by Commission Act of 1541* and the *Sedition Act of 1661* and declared them to be "utterly null and void to all purposes whatsoever" in the *Declaratory Act of 1766*.

Further, hereditary slave statutes and laws in colonial America impeded, hampered, or rescinded rights to which blacks born in the American colonies were entitled and enumerated in Parliament's *Habeas Corpus Act of 1679* and the *English Bill of Rights of 1689*. For example, unlawful detention, cruel and unusual punishment, and arbitrary imprisonment. Notwithstanding, and without lawful power and authority and in derogation of the "power and authority" of the Parliament, colonial assemblies throughout the American colonies, which include Virginia, Delaware, Maine, Georgia, Massachusetts, New Hampshire, Maryland, New York, New Jersey, North Carolina, Pennsylvania, South Carolina, Rhode Island, and Connecticut engaged in a pattern and practice of uttering pretended statutes and laws—which "denied" or "questioned" the "power and authority of the Parliament of Great Britain."

Moreover, six years later, in June 1772, the Court of the King's Bench's decision in the *James Somerset v. Charles Stewart* case struck down colonial slave statutes and laws... ruling that slavery was not "allowed and approved by the laws of this Kingdom," [46] and it also affirmed parliamentary sovereignty as it declared slavery cannot be a lawful condition if it is not allowed and approved by a "positive law," a power and authority only which Parliament possessed in the Kingdom.

When Lord Rockingham's ministry collapsed, the American colonies hoped that Parliament's changing Prime Ministers did not foretell pending financial consequences for the colonial leadership. Non-enforcement of the *Declaratory Act* had satisfied colonial America's leadership as they had no real view of how to address and resolve Parliament's exercise of parliamentary sovereignty legally. They knew enforcement would cause radical social changes throughout colonial America. Further, the lawmakers within the American colonies knew that it had unlawfully overrode multiple acts of Parliament during the period of salutary neglect and had created criminal exposure for their lawmakers and enslavers.

Likewise, it is essential to note that the spoke-and-hub conspirators within the American colonies knew the value of government corruption and alliances. They had operated freely within the American colonies and the Kingdom for a century, cultivated business relationships and friendships, and had powerful political connections throughout London. Once section II of the *Declaratory Act* created criminal exposure and personal challenges for the colonial elites and American lawmakers, most assuredly, their allies and supporters in London—British aristocrats—pro-slavery merchants, and their supporters within Parliament promised to foreclose the possibility of its enforcement within the American colonies which they still controlled.

Moreover, this relationship and assurance tapped down all potential fears and concerns within the American colonies about criminal prosecutions and radical social upheavals within the southern American colonies, and in becoming satisfied that it would not be enforced by the imperial government—the whole of colonial America was calm, compliant, and acted unaffected by section II of the Act. However, the failure of the imperial government to enforce the *Declaratory Act of 1766* or the Americans' misapprehension of the legal consequences of the Act during colonial times does not go toward the issue of its actual legal effect upon the American colonies—as it still abolished all repugnant colonial legislation, resolutions, votes, orders, and proceedings as a matter of law.

Section II of this act eviscerated these long-standing myths in 1766. It is reasonable to conclude that an objective interpretation will evidence that hereditary slavery was never legal since no colonial assembly could enact a slavery statute or law within the American colonies. Further, the Parliament of Great Britain "abolished" all pretended colonial "resolutions" and resulting hereditary slave statutes and slave laws enacted by the colonial assemblies in the American colonies because they "denied" or "questioned" Parliament's power and authority, which returned enslaved black colonials to status *quo ante*. <u>See</u> *Declaratory Act of 1766*.

Moreover—four years before the Declaration of Independence—England's Court of the King's Bench ruled in the *Somerset v. Stewart* case that slavery was not "allowed and approved by the laws of this Kingdom" and could only be a lawful condition by a "positive law." Colonial America's slave statutes and laws were judicially struck down, returning enslaved black colonials to the status *quo ante* under the English rule of law in 1772.

Parliamentary sovereignty was well-established, and the proof of its conclusiveness seemed unquestionable—as there were no examples of where the British courts had ever struck down an act of Parliament as unlawful or unconstitutional in 1766, and even if the Americans misapprehended Parliament's true intentions by this act, it is an irrelevancy as it became the law of the land.

The supreme power of the Parliament drove the Americans to believe that bringing legal proceedings in the British courts to challenge the *Declaratory Act of 1766* concerning section II of the act would be pointless. This sentiment and being assured by well-placed Londoners that the imperial government would not enforce the act caused all aggrieved party colonial assemblymen and enslavers within the American colonies not to challenge the *Declaratory Act of 1766*. The doctrines of the sovereignty of parliament and statutory interpretation were well-established principles during colonial times. [47] Moreover, all colonial governments within the American colonies and many aristocratic Englishmen were complicit and involved in the corruption of colonial government, graft, and colonial tyranny, which caused black colonials to be treated as personal property. These Englishmen were integral participants in the colony of Virginia's hub and spoke conspiracy and caused hereditary slavery to become endemic throughout colonial America.[48]

II. HISTORY OF THE COLOR-CONSCIOUS CONSTITUTION

The U.S. Supreme Court in *Dred Scott* did not suddenly imagine that Blacks had no rights that white men were bound to respect. In the book *Teaching White Supremacy*, scholar Donald Yacovone made the observation, "This principle was built into American society, and as the *Roberts* and the infamous 1857 *Dred Scott* cases showed, it dominated legal thinking, despite the later intentions of *Radical Republicans* in Congress and the new constitutional amendments." [49] Further, destructive to the notion of a color-blind constitution is parliamentary sovereignty, which Parliament exercised in March 1766 that abolished all legislative fiats based upon the *partus sequitur ventrem* resolution, votes, orders, and related proceedings that "denied" or "questioned" Parliament's power and authority.

For a good reason or no reason at all—this 1766 act of Parliament rendered all colonial slave statutes and negro laws "utterly null and void," as colonial assemblies within the American colonies pretended to overturn previous acts of Parliament. Thus, colonial slavery ceased to exist under the color of colonial statutes or laws exercised by colonial assemblies under parliamentary sovereignty in March 1766.

The accepted practice and the self-executing nature of section II of the *Declaratory Act of 1766,* when coupled with the Founding Fathers' grievance number 21 in the Declaration of Independence, which indicted the imperial government and King George III as a "tyrant"… for *"abolishing our most valuable laws, and altering fundamentally the Forms of our Governments."* could lead a conscientious observer to conclude that Parliament had indeed legislatively nullified "all colonial resolutions, votes, orders, and proceedings, in any of the said colonies or plantations, whereby the power and authority of the parliament of GREAT BRITAIN, to make laws and statutes as aforesaid, is denied, or drawn into question, are hereby declared to be, utterly null and void to all purposes whatsoever" by way of section II of that act in 1766 before our American patriots declared independence from Great Britain,[50] and the Founding Generation knew this to be the case.

The self-executing, sweeping, and provocative nature of parliamentary sovereignty leveled at the American colonies, given the unambiguous language used in Parliament's 1766 legislation, aligns perfectly with the Founding Generation's condemnation of the imperial government in the Declaration of Independence for abolishing "our most valuable laws, *and altering fundamentally the Forms of our Governments.*"

Further, it remains the most logical and practical conclusion that this grievance relates to section II of the *Declaratory Act of 1766*—and if the American patriots chose not to take advantage of this historic event to grieve to the King—the *Declaratory Act* of 1766, which purported to render "null and void" all repugnant colonial laws which included slavery laws and altering their governments—it would be pretty perplexing.

Historians claim that grievance number 21 in the Declaration of Independence relates exclusively to "*The Coercive Acts,*" which Parliament passed after "*The Boston Tea Party*" in 1774. [51] Those acts of Parliament were (1) The *Quartering Act of 1774,* which expanded upon the *Quartering Act of 1765*. It provided that the colonies had to provide barracks for British soldiers; (2) *The Administration of Justice Act* which allowed British officials accused of crimes in colonial America to be tried in Britain rather than in the colonies; (3) the *Boston Port Act* which closed the port of Boston to all ships until the colonists paid for the tea they dumped into the harbor; (4) *Massachusetts Government Act o*f 1774 which stripped the colony of Massachusetts of its charter and gave more power to the governor. Many of the government officials that used to be elected by the people would now be appointed by the governor. [52]

Significantly, grievance number 21 condemned King George III "*For taking away our Charters, abolishing our most valuable laws, and altering fundamentally the Forms of our Governments.*" However, carefully researching colonial America's history leading up to Parliament passing *The Coercive Acts* and reviewing the act reveals that "*The Coercive Acts*" in 1774 stripped the colony of Massachusetts of its colonial charter. While it fundamentally altered Massachusetts' government structure, the imperial government and King George III did not purport to abolish any "most valuable laws" in "*The Coercive Acts.*"

Secondly, if the American patriots' grievance number 21 in the Declaration of Independence relates exclusively to the *Massachusetts Government Act of 1774*, then it is duplicative and redundant since an earlier grievance indicted the imperial government and King George III for altering the Massachusetts charter to make judges and other officers independent of the people, and subservient to the Crown. [53]

Indeed, at first blush—this historical claim appears impossible to reconcile. Nonetheless, in deferring to the Declaration of Independence and historians—it would necessarily follow—that as the American patriots did claim in the Declaration of Independence that the imperial government and King George III did abolish colonial America's "*most valuable laws,*" it frames the question as to what act of the imperial government of Great Britain abolished their "most valuable laws" within the American colonies and, in effect, altered "fundamentally the Forms of our [their]

Governments," if not the "abolishing" of pretended colonial slave statutes and slave laws under the *Declaratory Act of 1766* since this act affected all thirteen colonies—not just the colony of Massachusetts.

Moreover, the *Dred Scott* decision ratified the ownership claims of white Americans over black colonials, and the ratification process established that the U.S. Constitution was never intended to create a color-blind constitution, [54] nor would such a constitution accurately reflect the social norms and mores of early America's society or present day. Thus, it is disingenuous, arrogant, and unfair for originalists and conservative jurists to propagate and use the myth of a color-blind Constitution to perpetuate the racial problems of a society that has failed to reach color-blind status.

Without regard to the Supreme Court's misapprehension of the law and facts, the *Dred Scott* case vanquishes this myth of a color-blind Constitution since the controversial case was never overturned, and the United States Supreme Court is the highest tribunal for all cases and controversies arising under the Constitution. As the final arbiter of the law, the Supreme Court is charged with ensuring equal justice under the law and, in *Dred Scott,* has already resolved whether the Framers of the Constitution contemplated a color-blind constitution.

The challenge for Scott, when he appeared before the U.S. Supreme Court, was that under the Constitution, and to bring the *de facto* habeas corpus lawsuit in the first place, one had to be a "citizen" and based upon the Declaration of Independence—the Supreme Court concluded that Scott was not a "citizen." Additionally, the Supreme Court concluded that Scott's status as a citizen of a free state did not necessarily give him status as a U.S. citizen. Taney concluded that while the states were free to create their citizenship criteria and had done so before the Constitution even came into being—the Constitution gave Congress exclusive authority to define national citizenship. The Court asserted, in general, that U.S. citizens were only members of the "political community" at the time of the Constitution's creation. Further, the Court asserted that even if Scott were deemed "free" under the laws of a state," he would still not qualify as an American citizen because he was black.

Moreover, the U.S. Supreme Court reasoned that the U.S. Constitution itself took slavery as a given in the fugitive-slave clause and the slave-trade clause, prohibiting Congress from passing legislation that would abolish the "migration or Importation of such Persons" before 1808 and allowing an import tax of up to "ten dollars for each Person." Taney took this as evidence that the country's founding documents did not confer on Black people "the blessings of liberty, or any of the personal rights so carefully provided for the citizen."

Additionally, the Supreme Court found that, in any case, Scott could not be defined as free by his residency in the Minnesota Territory because Congress lacked the power to ban slavery in U.S. territories. The

Court concluded that slaves were "property," and the Fifth Amendment prohibited Congress from taking property away from individuals without compensation. This, above all, was the "smoking gun" establishing a "color-conscious constitution," as the Supreme Court procedurally and substantively misapplied the English rule of law to arrive at this conclusion. Under the controlling English precedent of *R. v. Stapylton* (K.B. 1771), "being black will not prove the Property."

Firstly, and dispositive of the issue, England's *Magna Carta of 1215* and *Somerset v. Stewart* (K.B. 1772) mandated a due process hearing for the 500,000 black colonials. The U.S. granted no due process hearings to the Revolutionary War-era black colonials, and the legal issue as to whether such colonial black people and their descendants were members of the "political community" at the time of the Constitution's creation was never addressed by a court with competent jurisdiction.

Secondly, equally fatal to Taney's findings was that the *Declaratory Act of 1766* was self-executing, and this act of Parliament abolished all repugnant resolutions, votes, orders, and related proceedings in March 1766—which included all hereditary resolutions and negro laws throughout the American colonies because they denied or questioned the power and authority of Parliament. Parliament exercised its power and authority under parliamentary sovereignty and abolished all colonial-enacted slave statutes and negro laws in March 1766. Thus, white Americans did not legally own slaves when the Constitution was ratified. This act of Parliament in March 1766 was not repealed during colonial times.

Thirdly, the *Dred Scott* decision implicated the then 68-year-old legal dispute regarding the legal status of the 500,000 black colonials—first raised in May 1783 by British General Carleton to U.S. General Washington regarding the *Treaty of Paris of 1783*—before the Constitution was ratified in 1789. Despite assurances, 500,000 black colonials were denied fundamental due process rights under U.S. laws—and became the bedrock of America's slave-based economy.

After the Civil War, with the enactment of the Thirteenth,[55] Fourteenth,[56] and Fifteenth Amendments,[57] Congress had the opportunity to make the Constitution color-blind—but chose not to do so. Congressman Thaddeus Stevens offered language of total non-discrimination for these amendments, but Congress rejected comprehensive non-discrimination.[58] Further, the language Congress finally implemented in the amendments was Congressman Bingham's "Equal protection," which ensured the return of the Slave Codes in the guise of the Black Codes and the lengthy reign of the Jim Crow laws. Thus, it is clear that Congress did not seek a color-blind Constitution. [59]

In *Slaughterhouse Cases*, 83 U.S. 36 (1872), Louisiana passed a law restricting slaughterhouse operations to a single corporation. Under the law, this sole corporation received a charter to run a slaughterhouse downstream from the city. No other areas around the city were permitted for slaughtering animals over the next 25 years, and existing slaughterhouses would be closed. A group of butchers argued that they would lose their right to practice their trade and earn a livelihood under the monopoly. Moreover, they claimed the monopoly created involuntary servitude in violation of the Thirteenth Amendment, abridged privileges or immunities, denied equal protection of the laws, and deprived them of liberty and property without due process of law, violating the Fourteenth Amendment.

The Supreme Court issued a 5-4 decision finding that the Thirteenth and Fourteenth Amendment was only supposed to be applied "to the newly freed race," meaning African American men.

"[O]ne the most casual examination of the language of these amendments, no one can fail to be impressed with the one pervading purpose found in them all, lying at the foundation of each, and without which none of them would have been even suggested; we mean the freedom of the slave race, the security and firm establishment of that freedom, and the protection of the newly made freeman and citizen from the oppressions of those who had formerly exercised unlimited dominion over him." *Slaughterhouse Cases,* 83 U.S. (16 Wall) 36, 71 (1873).

Further, despite clear original congressional intent—it protected only rights that owed their existence to the federal government. All others fell to the states to enforce, with which, the Court ruled, the Fourteenth Amendment "had nothing to do." In his famous dissent, Stephen J. Field declared that his brethren on the Court had pulled off an extraordinary feat of legal magicianship, turning a constitutional amendment to aid newly freed African Americans into "a legal device to protect the most wealthiest and most powerful." Thus, this Supreme Court case strengthened *Dred Scott,* and this *Slaughterhouse Cases* decision was felt nearly one hundred years after it was decided. This case allowed the southern states to establish the doctrine of Separate but Equal using the same arguments made in the *Slaughterhouse* Cases.

In *Plessy v. Ferguson*, the Supreme Court upheld a Louisiana law that required segregation of black and white train passengers. The law at issue in Plessy was, in fact, genuinely color-blind on its face. The Louisiana law required that intrastate railroad passengers ride in train carriages with members of their race, thus denying the pleasures of diversity to African Americans and whites alike. When Plessy, seven-eighths white, attempted to sit in the passenger car reserved for whites and refused to move to the car "used for the race to which he belonged," he was ejected from the train and arrested by the New Orleans police.

According to the Court, the fact that the law did not conflict with the Thirteenth Amendment was "too clear for argument." [60] The Court found, however, that scrutiny of the law under the Fourteenth Amendment did not ban social distinctions based on race or demand "commingling upon terms unsatisfactory to either." Justice Brown then delivered the great lie of *Plessy*: segregative laws "do not necessarily imply the inferiority of either race to the other."[61]

In addition, in his dissent, Justice John Marshall Harlan predicted that the *Plessy* decision would eventually become as infamous as the Court's 1857 decision, *Dred Scott*, in which the Court ruled that black Americans could not be citizens under the U.S. Constitution and that its legal protections and privileges could never apply to them.[62]

III. BLACK ENGLISHMEN OF EQUAL SOCIAL AND POLITICAL RELATIONS

Anthony Johnson was one of the first Africans to arrive in the colony of Virginia. After serving as an indentured servant until 1635, he became free and a significant property owner... owning 250 acres of fertile land and holding five (5) indentured contracts by 1651. However, in 1652, "an unfortunate fire" caused "great losses" for Johnson, who was then married with two daughters. As was the practice, Johnson applied to Virginia's colonial court for tax relief. Without regard to Johnson's African origin, the colonial court granted his application for relief—evidencing that Africans who became free British citizens during colonial times had mainstream social and political relations under England's common law in early colonial America.

Further, during this time, taxes were levied on people, not property, as under the *Virginia 1645 Taxation Act* that provided... "All negro men and women and all other men from the age of 16 to 60 shall be tithable." However, on February 28, 1652, Virginia's colonial court exempted Johnson's black wife and two biological daughters, born in colonial Virginia, from paying taxes "during their natural lives." Virginia's colonial court exemption from taxation of the Johnson women gave them the same social status as white colonial women, who were not taxed in the colony of Virginia.

Then, in 1654, a civil replevin case captioned *Anthony Johnson v. Robert Parker*... this African immigrant prevailed in Virginia's colonial court. The case involved John Casor, a black indentured servant whose contract was owned by Johnson— but had been transferred to a white colonist named Robert Parker after Casor complained that his indentured contract had expired seven (7) years earlier and was being held illegally. Parker intervened on behalf of Casor and cajoled Johnson into freeing Casor since keeping indentured servants past their term of servitude was considered a severe offense. A person could be severely punished under England's common law. However, this was a scheme, as Casor had signed a lesser term of indenture in favor of Parker, but once the illiterate Johson discovered that Casor and Parker had conspired to defraud him. Johnson sought the return of Casor.

Initially, Virginia's colonial court ruled in favor of Parker. Still, after Johnson appealed in 1655, the colonial court's ruling was reversed. That tribunal found that Johnson still "owned" Casor's contract under England's common law and ordered Parker to return him to Johnson and required the losing Parker to pay court fees. In sustaining Johnson's claim against Parker, Virginia's courts established that black Englishmen and foreigners of African ancestry could bring lawsuits and claims in colonial America's courts under England's rule of law during colonial times.

Concurrently, in 1656, a colonial-born black woman, Elizabeth Key, was litigating a lawsuit in Virginia's colonial court and sought her freedom and that of her infant son. The core legal issue was the English common law doctrine of *partus sequitur patrem,* a father's status determined that of a newborn child. Thomas Key, Elizabeth's father, was a free white colonist. Secondly, she had been in indentured servitude for ten years longer than she should have: Thomas Key had stipulated that she was to be set free when she was fifteen.

Finally, she argued that she had been baptized as a child, was a practicing Christian, and should not be enslaved. She lost her case through an appeals court— where she petitioned Virginia's *House of Burgesses*, its colonial assembly, to investigate her case. A committee was formed to investigate, and they sided with Elizabeth, determining that she was free based on her father's status and baptism on July 21, 1656. This black English person became the first woman of African descent in the American colonies to sue for her freedom and win.

Anthony Johnson and Elizabeth Key's legal victories in colonial Virginia in the mid-1650s came at a formative moment in colonial America, as the concept of whiteness was emerging to reinforce existing power structures. Further, as Black people living in colonial America, both Johnson and Key are significant in that their legal, social, and political successes in the colony of Virginia predate the hardening of meaningful equal access and fair treatment under the rule of law for this ethnic group. Their treatment during the 1650s established equal legal, social, and political relations, making Johnson and Key's extremely significant because they symbolize a routine social status and ranking of people of African ancestry—a status and hierarchy that was practically and theoretically incompatible with a system of racial repression.

IV. VIRGINIA'S COLONIAL ASSEMBLY COULD NOT ENACT A SLAVE LAW

The bicameral structure of colonial legislatures within the American colonies prevented a colonial assembly from enacting a valid "positive law" without the assent of England's monarch. Moreover, the Virginia colonial assembly's matrilineal slavery scheme of *partus sequitur ventrem* "challenged" Parliament's power and authority to make laws throughout the Kingdom of Great Britain, as the *Royal Assent by Commission Act of 1541* and the *Sedition Act of 1661* were already the law of the land in 1662 when this hereditary slavery resolution was first introduced as being colonial law by Virginia's assembly.

Yet, Taney wrote in *Dred Scott* that the language of equality and rights "would not in any part of the civilized world be supposed to embrace the negro race, which, by common consent, had been excluded from civilized Governments and the family of nations, and doomed to slavery." The "unhappy black race," he observed, was "never thought of or spoken of except as property, and when the claims of the owner or the profit of the trader were supposed to need protection." This was historically inaccurate.

As Chief Justice Holt observed in *Smith v. Gould*, 2 Ld. Raym. 1274-75; 92 Eng. Rep. 499 (Q.B. 1706)... "The common law takes no notice of negroes being different from other men. By the common law, no man can have a property [interest] in another ..." Further, under English law—being bound by England's *Magna Carta of 1215* and its colonial charter, when the first nineteen kidnapped Africans who arrived in Virginia in 1619—they could only be indentured servants by law. In *Smith v. Browne & Cooper*, Chief Justice Holt ruled that "As soon as a negro comes to England, he is free; One may be a *villien* in England, but not a slave."

Bound by the English rule of law and colonial charter—no colonial assembly had the legal right, power, or license to decriminalize the kidnapping and enslavement of people within the American colonies. This was because of Parliament's *Royal Assent by Commission Act of 1541*, which made the formal assent of the English King a requirement to enact a valid colonial law, the *Sedition Act of 1661*, criminalizing the act of making laws without the assent of England's King and the *English Bill of Rights of 1689*. Bound by the English rule of law, hereditary slavery was a crime since "man-stealing," assault, and kidnapping were serious criminal acts under the English rule of law.

Secondly, Virginia's colonial assembly never had the lawful authority or power to enact a "positive law" to change the English common law doctrine of *partus sequitur patrem*, a father's status is the factor that determines a child's legal status into a matrilineal one and to enact a slave at birth regime within this British colony in 1662. Virginia's hereditary slave resolution denied and questioned parliamentary law. According to the colonial charter, Virginia's colonial assembly and all other colonial assemblies within colonial America were bound to honor and apply the English rule of law, which conferred British subjecthood unto all children born on British soil, prohibited slavery in the realm and the *English Bill of Rights of 1689* which protected fundamental liberty rights.

Thirdly, the colonial legislative structure in the colony of Virginia was bicameral, consisting of England's monarch as the upper house and, subsequently, the British Parliament and the colonial assembly headed by a colonial governor appointed by the British imperial government as the lower house. In being only one chamber of a bicameral legislative structure, Virginia's colonial assembly did not have the legal power or authority to enact a law derogating its grant of authority under England's constitution and the colonial charter. Moreover, England's King or authorized designee of the imperial government did not affirm Virginia's hereditary slave resolution. Lastly, Parliament criminalized the putative enactment of colonial "positive laws" under the *Sedition Act of 1661*. Consequently, these hereditary slavery laws enacted by colonial assemblies throughout colonial America were void *ab initio*.

But Virginia's colonial assembly had a secret weapon—Virginia's Royal Colonial Governor William Berkeley, who held his position because of who he knew rather than for what he could do. Those who benefitted from exploiting Africans and black Englishmen paid him to look the other way, and he complied. And Berkeley, in his capacity as colonial governor, conspired to prevent and foreclose further review of the hereditary slavery resolution before England's *Privy Council* or Court of the King's Bench—its highest court.

Governor Berkeley's failure to veto Virginia's slavery resolution was criminal malfeasance by omission. Further, Berkeley then committed malfeasance by commission by denying freedom to people of African descent after their term of indenture ended and barred further judicial review. Decidedly, Governor Berkeley engaged in racketeering and was critical in perfecting the criminal enterprise of hereditary slavery and was principally responsible for creating institutional racism, white supremacy dogma, and the spread of hereditary slavery throughout colonial America.

V. THE IMPERIAL GOVERNMENT ABOLISH DEFECTIVE COLONIAL LAWS

Dred Scott was the avatar of the existing social order and Blacks' position in the U.S. during the 1850s. Based upon colonial America's hub-and-spoke conspiracy, its evolved nature, and the U.S. Congress's failure to adhere to the rule of law concerning the legal rights of the 500,000 black Englishmen denied fundamental due process and then enslaved in the U.S. at the end of the American Revolution.

Taney's finding in the *Dred Scott* decision that African Americans were "regarded as beings of an inferior order, and altogether unfit to associate with the white race, either in social or political relations and so far inferior that they had no rights which the white man was bound to respect" was problematic as it gave total deference to the Framers of the U.S. Constitution. Following the original meaning of the Constitution necessarily means abandoning originalism. While most current Supreme Court justices use originalism in their legal reasoning, its use in the *Dred Scott* case is compelling evidence that originalism is too susceptible to selective reading of early American history and the difficulty attenuated to ascertaining the Framers' intent.

Judge Robert Bork, known as the "father of originalism," premised it as an answer to the problem of an unelected judiciary in a democratic system. However, Bork's answer is no solution, as originalist judicial review is just as incompatible with majority rule as non-originalism. Under both approaches, unelected judges rule on the constitutionality of actions by popularly elected officials.

Originalism answers that originalist judicial review is democratic because the people consented to adopt the Constitution, and originalism follows what was agreed to by ratification. Such a retort by originalists is factually inaccurate to say that "the people" consented to the Constitution because less than five percent of the population then participated in ratification. Moreover, no people of color or women participated, and only a small fraction of white men did. Furthermore, suppose originalists consider it undemocratic that our laws are subject to the approval of unelected judges. How much more undemocratic is it if society is governed by past majorities who ignored the rule of law and used the Constitution to ratify their enslavement of 500,000 legally free black Englishmen—twenty percent of the U.S. population during the 1780s?

The British imperial government protected hub-and-spoke conspirators operating in the American colonies and invented the white race in the late seventeenth century after *Bacon's Rebellion* in 1676.

Many historians point to *Bacon's Rebellion* in 1676, led by Nathaniel Bacon against Governor Sir William Berkeley when colonial America began distinguishing black people from white people. There were a great many reasons, all of which led to dissent in the colony of Virginia. Economic problems, such as declining tobacco prices, growing commercial competition from Maryland and the Carolinas, an increasingly restricted English market, and the rising costs of English manufactured goods, caused problems for the Virginians.

In 1675, a Potomac River planter named Thomas Matthew had a trade disagreement with a member of a native American tribe called Doegs. It escalated when Matthew and his neighbors killed several Doegs, which they claimed were attempting to steal livestock. The Doegs retaliated by killing an Englishmen. The local militia marched in pursuit. They followed the Doegs to their encampment and attacked them. Afterward, the militiamen came upon an encampment of peaceful Susquehannock hunters and attacked them. This action prompted a war with the Susquehannock, who raided frontier settlements and killed a dozen English settlers over the next few months. [63]

Governor Berkeley had long tried to balance his colonists' wishes against those of the native American tribes on Virginia's borders. But, his attempts to appease all sides failed, primarily when he used new trade rules to increase his wealthy friends' fortune. Bacon, who had recently arrived in Virginia and was Berkeley's cousin by marriage, was disgusted by what he viewed as the governor's disloyalty, dishonesty, and unfairness.

Bacon wanted the colonial government to retaliate for the raids by the Susquehannock on frontier settlements and to remove all Native Americans from the colony so landowners like himself could expand their property. Berkeley resisted, fearing that doing so would unite the nearby tribes in a costly and destructive war against the colony.

In response, and in defiance of the governor, Bacon organized his own militia, consisting of white and black indentured servants and enslaved black people, who joined in exchange for freedom and attacked nearby tribes. A power struggle ensued with Bacon and his militia on one side and Berkeley, Virginia's House of Burgesses, and the rest of the colony's elite on the other. Months of conflict followed—including armed skirmishes between militias. In September 1676, Bacon's militia captured Jamestown and burned it to the ground.

The events in Jamestown were alarming to the hub and spoke conspirators, the colonial government, and the planter elite class in the colony of Virginia. [64] The alliance between European indentured servants and people of African ancestry—indentured servants— Africans and free negroes caused a hardening of the racial caste regime in an attempt to divide the two races. Further, after *Bacon's Rebellion*, Virginia's lawmakers began to make legal distinctions between "white" and "black" colonials and created negro laws. They'd hoped that taking certain rights from black colonials and giving poor white indentured servants and farmers new rights and status would keep the groups separated and make it less likely that they would unite again in rebellion.

European values and traditions contributed to the vitality and acceptance of this white supremacy narrative within colonial America. Within this European tradition—darker-skinned people were universally stigmatized as laborers and servants, as it was a characteristic of most who worked outside in the sun and elements. Moreover, with the rise of a colonial-born black population within the British American colonies—those values, beliefs, and biases were seamlessly adopted by white colonists to support and perpetuate an informal race-based hierarchy entrenched throughout colonial America's social structures and institutions.

In the book *The Invention of the White Race*, Theodore W. Allen explained that his research of Virginia's colonial records did not reveal an official use of "white" as a token of social status before 1691. [65] This was not a matter of semantics; he also found that the "white race" as we know it was not, and could not, have been functioning in early Virginia. Over time, Virginia's policy of white-skinned privilege and the narrative that those unearned privileges entitled them to discriminate against any person and all people of African ancestry grew to influence social, political, legal, and labor systems throughout Atlantic World Societies.

The hub-and-spoke conspiracy organized by Virginia's colonial enslavers soon had a rim—the white colonials. But soon after Parliament passed the *English Bill of Rights in 1689* (declaring the rights and liberties of British subjects), the thought in colonial America became that the three distinct classes of blacks: (1) the free negro—one that was formally recognized as being free; (2) the colonial-born enslaved black—a black Englishman that was being criminally enslaved in derogation of the English rule of law and (3) the kidnapped African—an immigrant indentured servant held past the expiration of his indentured servitude contract had to be conflated, as the notion of the existence of a distinct class of black person called "free negro" and formally recognized as a free Englishman under the English rule of law was too great of a risk.

Such being the case, colonial enslavers created the colonial narrative—that being black was equal to being a slave, and the English rule of law protected none. This narrative caused colonial assemblies throughout the American colonies to pass countless colonial fiats designed to inhibit or foreclose black colonials' fundamental liberty and civil rights. The colonial assemblies did so at the behest of its colonial elite and slaveholders to protect wealth, political power, and their own liberty, as they were confident that the enumerated rights in the then newly enacted *English Bill of Rights of 1689* applied to all colonial-born enslaved blacks. The narrative conflated the three distinct classes of black colonials, and as poor whites were conferred more "white privilege," it proved effective, as the narrative subverted the legal status of the free negro and placed free negroes below the rule of English law.

It was Britain's first Prime Minister, Sir Robert Walpole's belief in 1721—"[I]f no restrictions were placed on the [American] colonies—they would flourish."[66] This period of governance came to be known as salutary neglect. Under this unofficial British policy, parliamentary rules and laws were loosely or not enforced on the American colonies and trade. For the colonists, this period of relaxation expanded freedom regarding trade and self-government. However, America's colonial assemblymen woefully abused its grant of legislative power by ignoring the English rule of law and the colonial charter by pretending to enact colonial slave statutes and negro laws, and resolutions without acquiring the assent of England's King or its imperial government as mandated by each of the colony's charter and the English rule of law.

Historians John E. Findling and Frank W. Thackeray, in their book—*Events That Changed America in the Eighteenth Century,* believed this "neglect" was not entirely deliberate and may have been caused by the British imperial government being overwhelmed and incompetent. Indeed, the vast ocean between England, the unchecked proliferation of a species of racial tyranny called hereditary slavery, and the American Revolution support this conclusion. This unofficial policy was in effect from 1607 to 1763.

The end of salutary neglect created an existential threat to colonial America's hub and spoke conspiracy in 1763 when the new Prime Minister George Grenville came into office. Grenville had placed a standing army in the American colonies against France's continued aggression at the end of the *Seven Years' War*. He also advocated for Parliament to enact laws requiring colonists to pay for the increased British troops. Grenville's rationale was that since the colonists in the American colonies benefitted from this deployment of soldiers, they should help pay for the army's cost through a series of taxes imposed by Parliament.

Parliament approved Grenville's proposal, including the *Stamp Act of 1765*. However, there was widespread opposition to the *Stamp Act* throughout the American colonies. The Americans claimed the act to be unjust, violated their rights as Englishmen to be taxed only by their consent through their representative assemblies, as had been the practice for a century and a half, and sought repeal of this act. Prime Minister Grenville and others were stunned by the level of opposition to the *Stamp Act,* which included riots and significant civil unrest. Parliament repealed the *Stamp Act* and passed the *American Colonies Act of 1766* (Geo. 3. C. 12), commonly known as the *Declaratory Act of 1766.*

The British imperial government's legislation in 1766 responded to Dr. Benjamin Franklin's insights regarding colonial legislative complaints and reasserted parliamentary sovereignty by legislating that Parliament could make laws binding the American colonies "in all cases whatsoever." Moreover, in section II of the *Declaratory Act*, Parliament exercised its supreme legislative authority and power by abolishing all pretended earlier repugnant legislative proceedings within the American colonies that violated parliamentary laws. This 1766 act of Parliament rendered colonial slave statutes and slave laws "utterly null and void" for "all intents and purposes whatsoever" since colonial slavery was based upon colonial assemblies' resolutions, votes, orders, and proceedings that "denied" and "questioned" Parliament's power and authority to pass laws within the Kingdom of Great Britain.

This act of Parliament was self-executing, and it is also counter-intuitive at best to conclude that this act enacted by the Parliament of Great Britain in March 1766—meant nothing despite its plain language that abolished legislative *all* colonial fiats based upon resolutions, votes, orders, and proceedings that "denied" or "questioned" its authority and power *inter alia* because the Americans did not protest section II of the *Declaratory Act*. The Supreme Court has clearly explained, "[I]n interpreting a statute a court should always turn to one cardinal canon before all others" . . . "Courts must presume that a legislature says in a statute what it means and means what it says there." *Connecticut Nat'l v. Germain*, 112 S. Ct. 1146, 1149 (1992).

Slavery within colonial America's thirteen colonies was extralegal during the early 1640s. However, in 1662, Virginia's colonial assembly passed a hereditary slave resolution titled *partus sequitur ventrem*—it was the product of a criminal conspiracy to exploit Africans and colonial-born black Englishmen who were the humblest of British subjects. Virginia's resolution decreed—that children of enslaved mothers, although born in the colony of Virginia and regardless of their father's race or status, would be born into slavery at birth. This colonial resolution "denied" and "questioned" the power and authority of the Parliament because Virginia's assembly did not bother to secure the Assent of England's King. Further, hereditary slavery denied colonial-born black Englishmen legal rights and protections authorized under England's *Magna Carta of 1215* and the *English Bill of Rights of 1689*.

Subsequently, all other colonies within colonial America enacted various hereditary slave statutes and negro laws, and none of those colonial assemblies bothered to secure the assent of England's King. All of the hereditary slavery resolutions and resulting legislation throughout the American colonies—no different than the colony of Virginia—"denied" and "questioned" the power and authority of the Parliament because colonial-born black Englishmen had legal rights and protections under England's *Magna Carta of 1215*, each colonial charter and the *English Bill of Rights of 1689*. Objectively, all thirteen colonial assemblies within North America "denied" and "questioned" the power and authority of the Parliament. [67]

Significantly, from the collapse of the centralized Dominion of New England in 1689 to 1763, salutary neglect was in effect. Britain began to try to enforce parliamentary laws, which also included the disallowment of laws to go into effect that were passed in colonial assemblies. Many historians agree that Grenville's *Sugar, Currency,* and *Stamp* Acts led to the American Revolution. The repeal of the *Stamp Act* allowed all Americans to rejoice. However, the

Declaratory Act forced many to reconcile, minimize their respective situation, and accept the state of play. Being assured that the imperial government would not enforce the act caused the rambunctious Americans to be conciliatory, raising no alarms and playing down the legal significance of section II in the *Declaratory Act*.

Moreover, most colonists presumed colonial legislation was lawfully enacted, and as few average colonists knew of the criminal scheme surrounding hereditary slavery—all ignored section II in the *Declaratory Act,* believing it to be superfluous. However, once Lord Chief Justice Mansfield, in the *Somerset* decision, six years later in 1772, struck down colonial slave statutes and laws, conditions changed within colonial America since he affirmed parliamentary sovereignty by declaring slavery within the Kingdom could only be authorized by a "positive law," a power and authority only which Parliament possessed. Mansfield's ruling reignited the financial and criminal concerns of colonial elites, colonial politicians, and enslavers within the American colonies in the run-up to declaring independence in July 1776.

Further, after the *Somerset* decision, colonial assemblies within the American colonies began seeking the King's assent on slave laws and resolutions, which he withheld. This resulted in several grievances being outlined in the Declaration of Independence. For example, grievance 1... *"He has refused his Assent to Laws, the most wholesome and necessary for the public good,"*... grievance 2... "He has forbidden his

Governors to pass Laws of immediate and pressing importance unless suspended in their operation till his Assent should be obtained, and when so suspended, he has utterly neglected to attend to them," and grievance 3... *"He has refused to pass other Laws for the accommodation of large districts of people unless those people would relinquish the right of Representation in the Legislature, a right inestimable to them and formidable to tyrants only."* White and black colonials held the same legal status under the English rule of law when the American colonies declared independence.

In *Marbury v. Madison*, 5 U.S. 137 (1803), America's renowned Chief Justice John Marshall ruled that: "[A] legislative act contrary to the Constitution is not law, [. . .] if two laws conflict with each other, the Courts must decide on the operation of each other, [. . .] Those, then, who controvert the principle that the Constitution is to be considered in court as a paramount law are reduced to the necessity of maintaining that courts must close their eyes on the Constitution and see only the law. This doctrine would subvert the very foundation of all written Constitutions. It would declare that an act which, according to the principles and theory of our government, is entirely void, is yet, in practice, completely obligatory. It would declare that if the legislatures shall do what is expressly forbidden, such act, notwithstanding the express prohibition, is in effect effectual. It would be giving to the Legislature a practical and real omnipotence with the same breath which professes to restrict their powers within narrow limits. It is prescribing limits and declaring that those limits may be passed at pleasure... Thus, the particular phraseology of the United States confirms and strengthens the principle, supposed to be essential to all written constitutions, that a law repugnant to the Constitution is void, and the courts and other departments are not bound by that instrument." *Marbury*, 5 U.S. at 137.

Parliament's abolishment of hereditary slave resolutions, votes, orders, and proceedings in 1766 and the facts determine whether white colonials and black colonials held the same legal status when the Founding Fathers declared America an independent nation in July 1776. The English rule of law also provided that a colonial government official's actions only have the force of law when that person acts within the rule of law. Moreover, when a government official acts without the imprimatur of any law, they do so by the sheer force of personal will and power. Thus, such actions are void *ab initio,* and in applying the British void *ab initio* doctrine regarding the colonial assemblies exercising putative legislative power—not granted to this inferior legislative body and especially vesting with the Parliament of Great Britain—the enactment of such slavery resolutions and slave laws never had the force of law. All parties were returned to status *quo ante* as a matter of law.

Centrally, one need only apply ordinary meaning to plain language in section II of the *Declaratory Act* of 1766 and do so in comparison to how Parliament construed a colonial resolution in its Examination of Dr. Benjamin Franklin before the House of Commons on

February 13, 1766, to conclude that "resolution" is the official name for colonial statutes and laws within the American colonies which Parliament intended to declare being "utterly null and void" in 1766. The language in the *Declaratory Act of 1766* is unambiguous and plain. Thus, in interpreting the simple language in section II of the *Declaratory Act* and Parliament's stated goal of reestablishing parliamentary sovereignty within the colonies in colonial America, all repugnant resolutions commonly referred to as statutes and laws within the American colonies that shared this same jurisdictional defect were rendered null and void as a matter of law.

Indeed, it would be both improper and a misnomer to call or describe pretended proceedings or sham instruments generated by a colonial assembly in the American colonies that issued without the King's "assent" and in furtherance of a criminal conspiracy to enslave countless innocent victims and violative of the English rule of law to be either a "law" or "statute" because colonial assemblies were not conferred legislative authority to enact a "positive law."

Doubtlessly, "It would be giving to the legislature a practical and real omnipotence with the same breath which professes to restrict their powers within narrow limits." *Marbury,* 5 U.S. at 137. Thus, Parliament only needed to nullify the discrete and integral aspects of the pretended statutes and laws, *i.e.,* resolutions, votes, orders, and proceedings to abolish colonial slavery. Moreover, it is doubly significant concerning pretended statutes and laws that denied colonial-born black

Englishmen legal rights and protections authorized under England's *Magna Carta of 1215* and the *English Bill of Rights of 1689*.

Under section II of the *Declaratory Act*—all legislative instruments generated within the American colonies to create the pretended slave statutes or laws— in the absence of the assent of England's King were effectively denying and questioning the power and authority of the Parliament—as they were legal nullities. This conclusion is very plain since all such instruments were legally inadequate to enact a "positive law" under the colonial charter—and as the colonial legislature was bicameral, with England's King, such instruments were "utterly null and void." Further, to enact a proper colonial law required both houses of the colonial Legislature to act in tandem and to be in accord—and without the imperial government's assent—none of the colonial assemblies' "proceedings" ever achieved the status of being a "statute" or "law."

Moreover, the colonial assembly could not be defined as being "a [properly constituted] legislative body," nor could its utterance be defined as "a written law" or "statute" enacted by a "legislative body." Thus, creating a fiction with the suggestion that these pretended instruments be referred to as a statute or law to be rendered null and void by this act of Parliament would be counter-intuitive and makes absolutely no sense. Moreover, rendering null and void "all resolutions, votes, orders, and proceedings, in any of the said colonies or plantations" had the legal effect of rendering invalid all "proceedings" ... and made them "utterly null and void to all intents and purposes whatsoever"—and it is the commonsensical abolishment of all pretended colonial slave statutes and laws that this Act sought.

The doctrine of colourable legislation is based on the Latin maxim: *Quando aliquid prohibetur ex directo, prohibetur et per obliquum...* "which states that what cannot be done directly should not be done indirectly." This doctrine has been used when a legislator oversteps its granted power and indirectly legislates on something it cannot do directly. The theory of colourable legislation evolved during the colonial times when self-government expanded its position in significant sections of the British Empire. *Cummings v. State of Missouri*, 71 U. S. 277 (1866) (ruling "the legal result must be the same if there is any force in the maxim, that what cannot be done directly cannot be done indirectly.")

And while conservative historians and others might still want to focus upon the fact that "statutes" and "laws" were not specially listed in section II of the *Declaratory Act of 1766,* it is black letter law that any such proponents bears—the burden of persuasion as to the existence of a properly executed hereditary slavery statute and slave laws in the first instance—none exists, and as "resolutions, votes, orders, and proceedings" are initial and integral aspects of this faux and vacuous claim of being a "statute" or "law," any such argument falters, as a matter of the English rule of law. [68]

Lastly, consistent with controlling English law during colonial times, and *Marbury*—repugnant colonial slave statutes and laws enacted (1) in derogation of the rule of English law and (2) were enacted in derogation of the colonial charter that required a colonial assembly to secure the assent of the imperial government never became law. *Marbury,* 5 U.S. at 137. These pretended statutes and laws were void *ab initio* and were of no legal consequence or effect. This is a dispositive fact and proposition. Moreover, as to whether the imperial government abolished colonial statutes and laws, the grievance section in the Declaration of Independence is corroborative proof as the Founding Fathers specially indicted King George III as being a tyrant *"for abolishing our most valuable* laws, *and altering fundamentally the Forms of our Governments."*

VI. THE JAMES SOMERSET HABEAS CASE

No statute codifying modern slavery was ever passed in England. The only forced labor recognized in English law was feudal *villeinage*, which had died out by the 17th century. Such was the reason why the original 19 Africans who arrived in the colony of Virginia in 1619 were treated as indentured servants—not slaves. Confusion arose when criminal elements within British colonies, which also started in Virginia, began a criminal enterprise called hereditary slavery in 1662.

In 1712, kidnapped Africans instigated a slave rebellion in New York City. At this time, the colony of

New York had one of the largest enslaved African populations of any of the thirteen colonies in North America. The Africans used the tenets of their religion to encourage black colonials to revolt—calling for a war on Christians. One out of every five colonists in the colony of New York was enslaved, and in not having plantations with large clusters of enslaved people—slavery in New York differed significantly from other colonies with large slave populations.

Most enslaved Africans were skilled workers—carpenters—stonemasons—fishermen, and boat builders. They lived and worked next to free blacks and indentured whites. There were unsupervised and unrestricted interactions between enslaved Africans and the other colonists. This engendered and normalized relationships, which became routine and commonplace since these inhabitants of New York City all lived in a small, dense area on the southern tip of Manhattan.

On the night of April 6, 1712, a group of more than twenty enslaved Africans gathered and set fire to a building on Maiden Lane near Broadway. While the white colonists were busy trying to extinguish the fire—the enslaved Africans, armed with guns, hatchets, and swords, attacked the whites and quickly fled. At least nine whites had been shot, stabbed, or beaten to death; another six were wounded. Afterward, white colonists arrested and jailed seventy people in the colony based on suspicion, and so goes the police report; while in custody and awaiting a trial—six Africans committed suicide.

Forty remaining prisoners were put on trial, eighteen were acquitted, and the rest were executed.

Responding to the *New York Slave Revolt of 1712*, all of the colonies in North America passed strict resolutions, restrictions, and codes on importing African-born people into the thirteen colonies and, in its stead, began an enhanced, robust, and systematic domestic breeding practice of enslaving colonial-born black Englishmen. This hub-and-spoke conspiracy initiative radically increased the number of enslaved people in colonial America, especially in the southern colonies with numerous breeding farms, and it boosted their profits.

This domesticated slavery initiative promoted coerced and forced sexual relations between males and child-bearing females as young as pre-teens to increase the number of enslaved people to meet projected future demands, anticipating the possible abolition of the *Atlantic Slave Trade*. The domestic breeding initiative in the aftermath of the *New York Slave Revolt of 1712* successfully increased the colonial-born slave population within colonial America. By the early 1770s, nearly a quarter of the population living in the American colonies were colonial-born people of African ancestry.

Doubtlessly, this misanthrope initiative of breeding colonial-born black people to be slaves within the American colonies during colonial times was a criminal practice, and all hereditary slave resolutions that authorized the enslavement of colonial-born violated several parliamentary laws. Further, colonial-born black

Englishmen were automatically returned to status *quo ante* under the English rule of law under the *Declaratory Act of 1766*. This act of the Parliament of Great Britain in 1766 rendered all pretended colonial slave "statutes" and slave "laws" enacted by colonial assemblies within the American colonies "utterly null and void" because colonial assemblies did not have the power and authority to enact a "positive slavery law." All such pretended slave "statutes" and slave "laws" were void *ab initio*. *Marbury*, 5 U. S. at 137.

  Lord Chief Justice Mansfield of the Court of the King's Bench issued a writ of habeas corpus and referred this case to its Twelve Judges procedure for a solemn decision, and so began the case of *James Somerset v. Charles Stewart* and the judicial review of colonial American slave laws. Significantly, this judicial review of colonial American slave laws concluded with a unanimous ruling of the twelve justices that found: "The state of slavery is of such a nature that it is incapable of being introduced on any reasons, moral or political, and instead, only by positive law, which preserves its force long after the reasons, occasion, and time itself from whence it was created is erased from memory. It is so odious that nothing can be suffered to support it but positive law. Whatever inconveniences, therefore, may follow from a decision, I cannot say this case is allowed and approved by the law of England, and therefore, the black must be discharged."

Mansfield announced the verdict of the Twelve Judges procedure, which judicially determined that American slave Laws—were legally defective since the tribunal found that slavery "must be recognized by the law of the country where it is used," slavery was an "odious" practice and "the state of slavery is of such a nature, that it is incapable of being introduced on any reasons, moral or political; but only [by] positive law." Only Parliament had the power and authority to enact a positive law within the Kingdom of Great Britain.

The *Somerset* decision created substantial criminal exposure for colonial elites, colonial politicians, and enslavers, as it had the legal consequence of striking down all pretended colonial slave statutes, laws, resolutions, votes, orders, and proceedings still operative within the colonial American colonies in 1772.

Further, the colonial assemblies in the American colonies had a bicameral legislative structure with England's King, which foreclosed any possibility of a colonial assembly enacting a positive law—since any putative slave law required the assent of England's King. None of the American colonies bothered to secure the assent of England's King on any of its pretended slave statutes and laws, and none had the power and authority to do so on its own. Moreover, England was a unitary State, and based upon this structure, only the Parliament held and wielded legislative power to enact a "positive law" to authorize slavery or to enslave colonial-born people at birth. [69]

The *Somerset* decision, when fastened to section II of the *Declaratory Act of 1766,* rendered all slave practices within the thirteen American colonies inert because England's highest court declared slavery could only be a lawful condition and practice within the Kingdom of Great Britain by a "positive law"—a legislative power which colonial assemblies never possessed or wielded and a legislative power which resided exclusively with the Parliament of Great Britain.

Legal historians such as Leonard W. Levy and Kenneth L. Karst opined in the *Encyclopedia of the American Constitution* that the *Somerset* decision of 1772 was controlling law within the American colonies as England's Court of the King's Bench specially analyzed colonial America's slave laws, statutes and in effect ruled that it was legally inadequate and could not enslave the colonial-born person called Somerset. Two years before the *Somerset* decision in *James v. Lechmere* (Mass.Superior Ct. 1770), a colonial court found the same as Lord Mansfield's conclusion but based upon English common law. Emory Washburn, *Sketches of the History of Massachusetts from 1630 to the Revolution in 1775*, Boston: Charles C. Little & James Brown (1840).

Legal scholar William M. Wiecek, in *Somerset: Lord Mansfield and the Anglo-American World,* misapprehended, overlooked, or ignored a critical legislative occurrence in July 1776 when he stated the *Somerset* decision "posed basic constitutional problems for the British imperial system, though these became irrelevant four years later with the declaration of

American independence." Continuing, Wiecek stated. . . "The question of Somerset's force under the imperial constitution became academic with the Declaration of Independence. Even if British courts or Parliament had been inclined to, they could not make policy for the independent American states." However, the British courts and Parliament did not have to make policy for the independent American states after the Declaration of Independence regarding the *Somerset* decision since one of the first legislative acts of the U.S. Congress was its adoption of Anglo-Saxon jurisprudence and the English common law in mid-July 1776.

Further, America's Congress did legislatively reject Thomas Jefferson's bill to supplant English law with Roman law. Congress also refused to disassociate this new nation from Anglo-Saxon jurisprudence, which occurred *after* the Declaration of Independence. Thus, the English rule of law and the *Somerset* decision created the same fundamental constitutional problems for America and its Constitution, which institutionalized slavery since it ratified "property" rights to America's slave-holding Founding Generation in legally free British subjects while denying such people basic due process guaranteed under the English rule of law.

Thus, the constitutional problems Dr. Wiecek observed that the *Somerset* ruling posed for the British imperial system did not become academic for the erstwhile British colonies with the Declaration of Independence and did soundly attach itself to the independent American states and its constitutionalism because *after* the Founding Generation declared themselves an independent nation in July 1776... America's first Congress formally adopted Anglo-Saxon jurisprudence (and *Somerset*), and England's common law became controlling precedent and law, and it still serves as the basis of America's jurisprudence today.

Significantly, colonial newspapers in the northern American colonies, such as the *Boston Gazette,* heralded:

"Emancipation came to English slaves when Mansfield, supposedly, declared that slavery was 'so odious, that nothing can be suffered to support it, but positive law' enacted by Parliament." However, England's Prime Minister North feared rebellion and the total breakdown in social order within the American colonies, so he directed colonial governors not to recognize the precedential effect of the *Somerset* decision. However, Lord North's directive caused northern colonials such as John and Samuel Adams of Massachusetts to clamor loudly that Prime Minister North's directive to its colonial governors evidenced England's blithe disregard for the rule of law as two successive colonial governors vetoed the legislative actions of the Massachusetts Assembly to liberate slaves in 1773 and 1774.

The Kingdom of Great Britain was "a nation of laws, not men." Thus, the unanimous ruling of His Majesty's King's Bench was the law of the land... slavery in colonial America ceased being "allowed and approved" throughout His Majesty's Kingdom as of June 1772, as a matter of the English rule of law. Lord Mansfield's judicial ruling, when coupled with Parliament's *Declaratory Act of 1766* that legislatively nullified all repugnant colonial slave statutes, laws, resolutions, and orders, had, in effect—outlawed slave practices within the American colonies.

While slave-owning Englishmen in the southern colonies, such as George Washington, Thomas Jefferson, James Madison, John Marshall, and others, were quite pleased with Lord North's directive as colonial elites, colonial politicians, and enslavers were convinced that the enforcement of the *Somerset* decision within the American colonies would financially ruin them and the colony. The gravity of the circumstances caused Virginia's slaveholders to surmise and reason that a combined committee of all 13 colonies needed to be formed to aid them in defending their wealth. However, there were no established lines of communication between regional governments since the British imperial government discouraged it. However, in the spring of 1773, the colonists in Massachusetts began to complain that they were being taxed without representation, and this unrest created an opportunity for the Virginians to establish a line of communication in the northern colonies.

The future of slavery after the *Somerset* decision was the catalyst that drove the thirteen American colonies to organize. However, the founding generation knew that the privileged class's resistance to British governance and its ruling on the question of slavery that delivered them riches was a problematic rallying cry to mobilize the masses to the point of rebellion. This reality caused colonial America's patriots to frame their quarrel with England as being based upon the natural rights of all colonial subjects and common welfare, giving rise to the notion that governments derived, or ought to derive, their authority from the consent of the governed. The Founding Generation then adopted the political philosophies of liberalism and republicanism, claiming all men were created equal.

VII. AMERICA'S DECLARATION OF INDEPENDENCE

The Declaration of Independence, drafted by Thomas Jefferson, was debated and revised by the entire U.S. Congress. In the last public letter he wrote before he died in 1826, Jefferson called the Declaration "an instrument, pregnant with our own and the fate of the world," as he declined an invitation to attend the commemoration in Washington, D.C., on the fiftieth anniversary of American independence according to noted historian David Armitage's, *The Declaration of Independence: A Global History* which examined how this historic 18th century document became a political and philosophical model for nations and people across the globe. [70]

According to Armitage, the Declaration of Independence was a document of international law, influenced by Emerich de Vattel's *The Laws of Nation*,

Or, Principles of the Law of Nature, Applied to the Conduct and Affairs of Nations, a work of political philosophy and international relations. Declaring America independent was a necessary first step if the emerging nation was to have any hope of attaining the recognition it sought from the European powers. Armitage supported this conclusion by observing that "Vattel made independence fundamental to his definition of statehood," the primary purpose of the Declaration was "to express the international sovereignty of the United States." However, in being recognized as a sovereign nation—the U.S. fastened itself to universally accepted principles of international traditions, decorum, and international law.

Jefferson did not carve black colonials out of the Declaration. Moreover—when he wrote "all men are created equal" in the preamble of the Declaration—he was not talking about individual equality. Instead, Jefferson was advancing the view that the American colonists, as a people, had the same rights of self-government as other peoples and, hence, could declare independence, create new governments, and assume their "separate and equal station" among other nations. Further, Jefferson's opinion of the *Declaratory Act* was That "By one act they have suspended the powers of one American legislature and by another have declared they may legislate for us themselves in all cases whatsoever. These two acts alone form a basis broad enough whereon to erect a despotism of unlimited extent."

The grievance section of the Declaration reveals the actual and legal significance of not having the assent of England's King affixed to their hereditary slave "resolutions, votes, orders, and proceedings" passed by colonial assemblies as it highlights... that the first three grievances listed is that *"He [King George III] has refused his Assent to Laws, the most wholesome and necessary for the public good,"* ... Secondly, *"He has forbidden his Governors to pass Laws of immediate and pressing importance unless suspended in their operation till his Assent should be obtained; and when so, has utterly neglected to attend to them."* Thirdly, *"He has refused to pass other Laws for the accommodation of large districts of people unless those people would relinquish the right of Representation in the Legislature, a right inestimable to them and formidable to tyrants only."*

Moreover, grievances eight and nine in the Declaration of Independence stated, *"He [King George III] has obstructed the Administration of Justice, refusing his Assent to Laws establishing judiciary powers"* and "He had made judges dependent on his Will alone, for the tenure of their offices, and the amount and payment of their salaries." It supports the legal conclusion that the colonial assemblies did not have the power and authority to enact resolutions, votes, orders, and related proceedings without securing approval from England's King. And in this regard, the Declaration is compelling evidence.

The significance of having the King's assent unto colonial laws becomes self-evident as the Founding Fathers were concerned that their pretended slave statutes and slave laws had been rendered "utterly null and void" by Parliament's *Declaratory Act of 1766* since colonial assemblies did not secure the "assent" of the imperial government or England's King upon colonial legislative slavery fiats based upon the hereditary slave resolution *partus sequitur ventrem* which specifically denied and questioned Parliament's *Sedition Act of 1661* and the *English Bill of Rights of 1689.*

Additionally, the grievance section indicted King George III for *"abolishing our most valuable laws."* Yet, various historians resist the legal conclusion that the Founding Fathers were complaining about Parliament's *Declaratory Act of 1766,* which abolished colonial laws. However, and without regard to the reasonableness of this legal conclusion—it necessitates establishing the exact abolished colonial laws that the Founding Fathers were referencing in the Declaration and under what legislative act of the imperial government—if not Parliament's *Declaratory Act of 1766.*

Doubtlessly, the Founding Fathers conceded Parliament's power and authority and accepted the abolishment of all repugnant statutes, laws, and other legislative proceedings concerning black colonials. In furtherance, three grievances support this conclusion. In this regard, grievance twenty blames King George III "For abolishing the free Systems of English Laws in neighbouring [sic] Province, establishing therein an

Arbitrary government, and enlarging its Boundaries so as to render it at once an example and fit instrument for introducing the same absolute rule into these Colonies," ... grievance twenty-one "*For taking away our Charters, abolishing our most valuable laws, and altering fundamentally the Forms of our Governments,*" and grievance twenty-two "For suspending our own Legislatures, and declaring themselves invested with power to legislate for us in all cases whatsoever."

These grievances in the Declaration of Independence in 1776 would lead a conscientious reader to review colonial slave statutes, laws, resolutions, orders, and other legislative proceedings to determine and discern whether all or none had the assent of England's King. This is a threshold inquiry that the Supreme Court in the *Dred Scott* case did not do.

In the colony of Virginia, Jefferson lived in a planter economy dependent upon slavery and, as a wealthy landholder, used slave labor for his household, plantation, and workshop. He first recorded his slaveholding in 1774 with 41 enslaved people. [71] Having been assigned to write the Declaration of Independence, Jefferson condemned the slave trade. He criticized King George III for supposedly forcing slavery onto the American colonies in his draft of the Declaration of Independence, which was stricken by other Southern delegates.

Jefferson feared the *Declaratory Act of 1766 and* stated: "By one act they have suspended the powers of one American legislature and by another have declared they may legislate for us themselves in all cases whatsoever. These two acts alone form a basis broad enough whereupon to erect a despotism of unlimited extent." Moreover, encouraged and supported by his teacher of the law, Judge George Wythe, Jefferson concluded that hereditary slavery would be an unworkable institution in this new nation under Anglo-Saxon jurisprudential doctrines and England's common law. He pushed the U.S. Congress to supplant English law with Roman law. However, Jefferson and his supporters were unsuccessful as Congress formally adopted the English rule of law for the United States of America in July 1776.

In 1784, Jefferson proposed the abolition of slavery in all western U.S. territories and limiting slave importation to 15 years. Further, Jefferson wrote of his "suspicion" that black people were mentally and physically inferior to Whites. Still, he argued that they had innate human rights and that slavery was a moral evil for which the nation would ultimately have to account to God. [72] Yet, during his presidency, Jefferson was mainly publicly silent on slavery and emancipation, as the Congressional debate over slavery and its extension caused a dangerous north-south rift among the States, with talk of a northern confederacy in New England. [73]

In 1787, when Jefferson took a 13-year-old black English child, Sally Hemings, to Paris, France, he knew his slave ownership claim of this colonial-born child, his sister-in-law, who, according to scholarly consensus, came to father at least six children with her, was without merit since Parliament abolished all hereditary slavery resolutions, votes, orders, and proceedings in 1766 and six years later in 1772, Lord Chief Justice Mansfield ruled in the *Somerset* case that the institution of slavery was not "allowed and approved by the laws of this Kingdom." This enlightened and informed man of the Eighteenth century, learned in law and politics, knew that he was persecuting a free but uninformed and powerless black child—but did not care.

The claim that Hemings was born legally free in the colony of Virginia in 1773 is fastened to the self-executing nature of the *Declaratory Act of 1766* that abolished Virginia's *partus sequitur ventrem* resolution because this hereditary slavery resolution enacted in 1662 denied and overruled Parliament's *Royal Assent by Commission Act of 1541* and *Sedition Act of 1661* that bound colonial assemblies to secure the King's assent on all resolutions, votes, orders, and proceedings enacted in throughout the Kingdom. Virginia's *House of Burgesses* did not bother to secure the King's assent on this 1662 hereditary slavery resolution. Moreover, the decision of the Court of the King's Bench in the *Somerset* case found slavery was "odious" and unconstitutional under English law—the year before Hemings was born in the colony of Virginia.

In being a crown colony, Virginia was bound by its colonial charter to the English rule of law and the unanimous decision of His Majesty's King's Bench, which oversaw Britain's *Privy Council*. This *Somerset* decision required no ancillary legislation nor intervening court action. The *Somerset* decision did not need to be ratified by the colony of Virginia to be controlling law. The *Somerset* decision was the law of the land in British colonial America.

Even more disturbing, admirers of Jefferson are willing to give him a free pass, classifying him as an enlightened slave owner who treated his slaves well and sought to emancipate some. For example, he purchased some slaves to reunite their families and did not work his slaves on Sundays and Christmas, and he allowed them more personal time during the winter months. However, some scholars doubt Jefferson's benevolence, noting cases of excessive slave whippings in his absence. [74]

Further, it is claimed that Jefferson felt slavery was harmful to both slaves and enslavers. However, despite knowing that all Revolutionary War-era blacks were entitled to liberty under the *Treaty of Paris of 1783*, he did not release these black Englishmen from captivity—while advocating for gradual emancipation. Further, during the *Revolution* in 1779, Jefferson proposed gradual voluntary training and resettlement of colonial slaves to Virginia's assembly, and three years later, he drafted legislation allowing slaveholders to free their black slaves. However, over Jefferson's lifetime, he owned 600 enslaved black people, and other than Hemings' children, he released few, which amounts to "slave-splaining" or an attempt to explain or lessen slavery's dehumanization and degradation.

Moreover, core to Jefferson's free pass is the ahistorical notion that the blacks—he lorded over were legal slaves under the English rule of law. But it is inaccurate—as Jefferson professed lordship over legally free black Englishmen under the English rule of law, adopted by the U.S. Congress.

This was the case since slavery in colonial America was an extralegal practice—perpetrated due to the corruption of colonial government enacting repugnant colonial laws, which the British imperial government abolished in 1766 since colonial America's "most valuable [hereditary slavery] laws" purported to override parliamentary laws and were even chronicled as grievances in Jefferson's draft of the Declaration of Independence in 1776. However, the most egregious aspect was that Jefferson stood mute.

Jefferson was chosen in 1782, along with Dr. Benjamin Franklin, John Jay, Henry Laurens, and John Adams, to negotiate the terms for peace with the British, resulting in the *Treaty of Paris of 1783*. At the same time, after the ratification of the treaty in January 1784 and the U.S. Congress being fully aware of the fact that the British were claiming liberty for all black colonials in accordance to the English rule of law—500,000 black Englishmen were denied the fundamental right of due process of law and made the bedrock of America's slave-based economy—a searing affront to the foundational ideals of the American experiment—no one is above or below the rule of law and for which so many had given their lives: yet, Jefferson who benefitted his entire life from this misanthropic and fraudulent practice said nothing.

In the book *Fallen Founder: The Life of Aaron Burr*, Nancy Isenberg observed, "These were our founders: imperfect men in a less than perfect nation, grasping at opportunities. That they did good for their country is understood; that they were also jealous, resentful, self-protective, and covetous, politicians should be no less a part of their collective biography. What separates history from myth is that history takes in the whole picture, whereas myths avert our eyes from the truth when it turns men into heroes and gods."

Sardonically, it is Jefferson's self-promotion to the status of a leader of "a nation of laws, not men" and the ideal that "all men are created equal" that prevents this founder from being described as mere "imperfect men." Jefferson dehumanized countless black men, women, and children to further these ideals of a "more perfect union." He did so "on the backs" of foreign nationals and violated international traditions. The misanthropic enslavement of black Englishmen and the denial of the fundamental right to due process of law prevents him from being granted a free pass.

VIII. AMERICA'S REVOLUTION AND SLAVERY

The Twelve Judges conducted a judicial review of American slave laws in connection with addressing Somerset's petition for liberty and declared slavery was not "approved and approved by the laws of this

Kingdom" in 1772. All badges of legality were withdrawn from this misanthrope practice. Slavery laws within the American colonies became void *ab initio*, and the *Somerset* decision was the seminal event that gave rise to the creation of the *Continental Congress*, as it exposed seeded trust issues by and between England's King George III's colonial governors and their hub and spoke co-conspirators and enslavers residing in the southern colonies. Further, it gave the colonies a common grievance to unite them against the British imperial government: mishandling the *Somerset* decision in colonial America created impetus for rebellion in 1772.

In the book *Slave Nation: How Slavery United the Colonies and Sparked the American Revolution*,[75] the historians observed that the southern colonial elite had two concerns regarding the *Somerset* decision—one—they worried enslaved Americans would hear about the *Somerset* decision and try to escape to England where they would be declared free according to Lord Chief Justice Mansfield's *Somerset* decision precedent and—two—colonial slavery was ending due to a secretive and undisclosed emancipation initiative led by the imperial government. But in truth, there was only one concern—they worried about being disgraced, impoverished, and imprisoned in England once the imperial government enforced the English rule of law in colonial America.

The colonial planter, enslavers, and lawmakers were learned and Enlightened men who knew to a legal certainty that chattel slavery was a criminal racket, as the imperial government had stripped away their façade of legitimacy by way of the *Declaratory Act* in 1766 and now, six years later—the *Somerset* decision. Fortunately for these colonials—many powerful and influential people in London stood to lose massive wealth along with them if the imperial government enforced the *Somerset* decision—since the underlying hereditary slave fiats were already null and void based upon the resolution of *partus sequitur ventrem* denied and questioned the power and authority of Parliament.

Further, the *Somerset* decision was self-executing, and as the Court of the King's Bench had original jurisdiction over the American colonies and was the highest court in the Kingdom—no legal options existed. No other court in the Kingdom contemplated that the King was permanently presiding. [76] However, the imperial government directed the colonial governments within the American colonies not to enforce the *Somerset* decision in colonial courts.

The imperial government fashioned and advanced the narrative that the unanimous *Somerset* decision of the Court of the King's Bench of twelve justices only meant "a person, regardless of being a slave, could not be forcibly removed from England against his will and carried him abroad."

The *Somerset* decision was a controlling precedent overruling all life-long slavery verdicts and colonial slave laws. This ruling declared that only

Parliament had the power to authorize slavery in the Kingdom, and it did not. The King's Bench reaffirmed parliamentary sovereignty and, in effect, struck down all colonial American slave statutes and laws since "positive law" was defined as "law actually and specifically enacted or adopted by proper authority for the government of an organized jural society." Under each colonial charter within colonial America, the proper authority to enact a "positive law" in the American colonies was vested with the Parliament of Great Britain—not a colonial assembly.

In the modern context, His Majesty's highest tribunal—the Court of the King's Bench in the *Somerset* case, ruled by a unanimous decision that slavery was unconstitutional throughout the British Empire and struck down all forms of *de facto* slave statutes, laws, customs, and practices within the American colonies. The *Somerset* decision returned black colonials suffering as slaves in the American colonies to the status quo ante—since colonial slavery was always an extralegal practice. Thus, as colonial slavery—their wealth, social status, and liberty were now wholly dependent upon corrupt British officials' grit, whim, and caprice—the Americans in the southern colonies knew thunderclouds were gathering three thousand miles away in London.

Dutifully, Massachusetts Governors Thomas Hutchinson and Sir Thomas Gage followed the imperial government's non-enforcement directive regarding the *Somerset* decision in colonial courts. However, they also each had occasion to veto the Massachusetts Assembly's legislative actions favoring the emancipation of the colony's slaves in 1773 and 1774. The imperial government was concerned that the Massachusetts Assembly's legislation might spread and void its non-enforcement directive within colonial courts and their status quo protection narrative and thus destroy the financial underpinning of the southern colonies and cause rebellion.

King George III's ministers knew, as did the southern colonial elite and the men of the Massachusetts Assembly, that the colonial governors' failure to enforce the English rule of law did not change or alter its legal consequence, as the Somerset decision was self-executing, required no affirmative actions on the part of any colonial official. All colonies were bound by their charters, whether a crown or a proprietary colony, to adhere to the rule of law announced by His Majesty's highest court: the Court of the King's Bench.

Northern patriots, such as Samuel Adams, clamored that the vetoes of the Massachusetts Assembly's legislative actions to liberate slaves—by successive colonial governors evidenced Britain's blithe disregard for the rule of law announced in the *Magna Carta of 1215* and the *Somerset* decision—proving corruption and colonial government tyranny. While patriots in the southern colonies like the Virginian James Madison were pleased by the Massachusetts Governors Hutchinson and Gage's vetoes—he and his cohort believed the imperial government's handling of the hereditary slavery issue foretold of a nefarious plot to rob them of their wealth—generational wealth created from the criminal enslavement of native-born black subjects of His Majesty, including their value as capital and the value of what they produced, even their children.

Ever so mindful that they were handsomely compensating southern colonial governors, local officials, and others—the southern colonial elite in each of these colonies were highly dissatisfied with the state of affairs of their colonial slave enterprise as they were paying for protection. Further, given Parliament exercising parliamentary sovereignty and its abolishment of their hereditary slave resolution of partus sequitur ventrem under the *Declaratory Act* and now the *Somerset* decision—it caused them to believe their tributes to colonial governors and London lawmakers were wasteful. Their concerns were well-founded since the *Somerset* decision struck down all colonial slave laws, and as self-executing, it was the law of the land. Also, the King could no longer just wave his scepter and guarantee the continuation of hereditary slavery—the unbridled power of the Crown had long since been substituted with the *English Bill of Rights of 1689*. The *English Bill of Rights* was an act of Parliament that guaranteed certain rights of the subjects of England and limited the power of the Crown.

The southern colonial American elite, who profited from chattel slavery, knew that if the imperial government saw fit, it had the power to determine that hereditary slavery ended in 1766 and forcefully liberate colonial blacks suffering as slaves throughout colonial America. They felt it to be more likely now since Britain's highest court determined the *Somerset* decision. If this happened, they would have no legal options since Parliament rendered all colonial hereditary slave resolutions, votes, orders, and proceedings "utterly null and void." Hereditary slavery was unlawful as the practice violated England's *Magna Carta of 1215* and the *English Bill of Rights of 1689*. Parliament's adoption or recognition of the *Somerset* decision would financially ruin many—virtually destroying colonial America's economy and creating criminal exposure and possible criminal prosecutions for all enslavers within the American colonies.

Alternatively, those that profited from chattel slavery believed that even if Parliament was reluctant to lose the benefit of the revenue generated from colonial America's slave-based economy, it might still preserve chattel slavery and seek to fill Britain's treasury by taxing slaves, slave masters, or colonial exports. Everyone that owned slaves in colonial America felt that any of these scenarios would decimate and potentially destroy their wealth.

The gravity of the circumstances regarding colonial slavery caused Virginia's colonial elite to surmise that a combined committee of all colonies needed to be formed to aid them in defending their wealth. However, there were no established lines of communication between regional colonial governments since Britain discouraged it. However, soon after that, the Virginians came to recognize the regional civil unrest in the colony of Massachusetts as an opportunity to establish a line of communication within the northern colonies.

The colony of Virginia's colonial governor, Lord Dunmore, was governing the colony without convening its colonial assembly as the *Somerset v Stewart* habeas case was proceeding before the Court of the King's Bench in London, England. There were tense relations between himself and Virginia's colonial assemblymen. Still, His Lordship found it necessary to pause the suspense of Virginia's colonial assembly and convene this legislative body in March 1772, when he came to need funds to finance his campaign against Native Americans known as *Lord Dunmore's War*. In recess, Virginia's assemblymen had no legislative authority—no power under Virginia's colonial charter. Virginia's assemblymen had legislative power only when Virginia's governor elected to convene the body. However, after Lord Dunmore convened the legislative assembly—instead of dealing with the funding issue, the Virginian assembly resolved to form a committee to communicate concerns about the *Townshend Acts* and the *Gaspee Affair*. In the spring of 1773, the colonists in Massachusetts complained that a British subject's property in the form of taxes could not be taken from him without his consent, in the form of government representation, and that since that had no representation in Parliament, the colony should pay no taxes. The slogan expressed this view: "No taxation without representation." Parliament's lack of colonial representation was a common denominator and was viewed by all within colonial America as political corruption and imperial governmental tyranny.

In May 1774, the British imperial government exacerbated colonial discontent in the colony of Massachusetts when Parliament passed the *Massachusetts Acts of 1774*, referred to as the *Coercive Acts of 1774*. This act of Parliament closed the Port of Boston—sent in troops of occupation—appointed a military governor for the colony of Massachusetts, and, as if a British official could not get a fair trial in Massachusetts—allowed the governor to order a trial of an accused royal official to take place in England. These acts by the imperial government were capitalized upon by Virginians such as George Washington, who called this the *"Murder Act"* because he believed that it allowed British officials to harass Americans and then escape justice, which radicalized northern colonies and went a long way in dispelling lingering thoughts and illusions about colonial American's rights and status as Englishmen.[77] This allowed the Virginians to embed themselves and aid in Massachusetts' cause.

With their secreted agenda, members of Virginia's committee successfully lobbied other southern colonies to join a *Continental Congress* committed to their universal protection and the furtherance of hereditary slavery. However, when the British imperial government became aware of the Virginia committee's actions—which included bankrolling the vexatious rebellion in the colony of Massachusetts with skills, resources, and money they had amassed from chattel slavery and their structuring of the *Continental Congress*—their century-long partnership with America's patriots in the southern colonies splintered.

Virginia's governor, Lord Dunmore, reconvened Virginia's House of Burgesses during the spring of 1774 to address public safety issues. However, he quickly dissolved the body again when Virginia's colonial assemblymen passed a resolution declaring June 1, 1774... a day of fasting and prayer in the colony of Virginia. Afterward, Lord Dunmore declared martial law. However, Virginia's colonial assemblymen without legal rights, authority, or privilege—purported to reconvene Virginia's Assembly as the Second Virginia Convention and did elect delegates to the *Continental Congress*. The act of reconvening Virginia's Assembly was done without legal authority, violating the English rule of law.

Swiftly, Lord Dunmore issued a proclamation denouncing the process, the actions of Virginia's assemblymen, and the credentials of Virginia's delegates to the *Continental Congress*. However, these people took seats in the *Continental Congress* with nullified and withdrawn credentials and became instrumental in drafting and voting on the final version of the Declaration of Independence.

In its aftermath, rumors of a British plan to enforce the *Somerset* decision and draft formerly enslaved people into the military began circulating to such an extent within the colony of Virginia that a group of enslaved people presented themselves to Virginia's governor to volunteer their services the following April. Lord Dunmore delayed the decision by ordering them away, but the suspicions of Virginia's conspirators and slave masters were not allayed. Much of the literature and newspaper reporting out of London supported their suspicions, as rumors swirled that an emancipation bill of the American colonies was set to reach the floor of the British Parliament—which did not materialize until the *Slave Trade Act of 1807*.

By the spring of 1775, the tension between England and the *Continental Congress* had escalated, and it caused an order to be given to all colonial governors to secure all gunpowder to deprive potential rebels of this crucial military supply. Lord Dunmore complied on April 21, 1775, ordering Lieutenant Henry Colins, commander of HMS *Magdalen,* to remove the gunpowder from the public magazine in Williamsburg. The officer removed fifteen half-barrels and transported them to a British warship, provoking what became known as the *Gunpowder Incident*. Having been the governor of New York before being appointed governor of Virginia, Lord Dunmore was aware of the colonists' fear of insurrections, and when they confronted him—believing he had acted to expose them to their slaves, he repeatedly threatened to free and arm slaves to defend the cause of England's imperial government. He was confident that the threat of armed former slaves running throughout the colony of Virginia and, in exchange, them conceding a few barrels of gunpowder would be an acceptable bargain for the colonists. Lord Dunmore was wrong.

On May 3, 1775, the Hanover Militia, led by Patrick Henry, arrived outside Williamsburg. This caused Lord Dunmore to abandon the Governor's Palace for his hunting lodge in Porto Bello in nearby York County. His Lordship then proclaimed on May 6, 1775, against "a certain Patrick Henry" ... and "a number of deluded Followers" who had organized "an Independent Company... and put themselves in a Posture of War." Lord Dunmore threatened to impose martial law. Subsequently, members of Virginia's militias laid siege to Lord Dunmore's hunting lodge, wounding him in the leg and forcing him to flee aboard the man-of-war ship HMS *Fowey* in the York River.

Over the following months, Lord Dunmore sent many raiding parties to plunder plantations along the James, York, and Potomac rivers, particularly those owned by rebels. The raiders exacerbated tensions since they not only took supplies, they also encouraged black slaves to rebel, and on November 7, 1775, Lord Dunmore formally declared "all indented servants, Negroes, or others... free that are able and willing to bear arms." Dunmore's proclamation was well-publicized, and enslaved Black people throughout the thirteen colonies separated themselves from their masters to join the British. Dunmore's proclamation was an iteration of the British *Southern Strategy* envisioned by King George III's ministers to quell rebellion and devastate colonial America's economy by causing chaos in the southern colonies and weakening or splintering the *Continental Congress*.

Colonial newspapers published Dunmore's Proclamation in full. However, the *Virginia Gazette* warned the enslaved to " Be not then... tempted by the proclamation to ruin your selves." Continuing, the newspaper urged enslaved blacks to "cling to their kind masters," as it claimed—Dunmore's proclamation was only a ploy—but it did not work since blacks from all the American colonies were leaving their masters in pursuit of freedom. Under the English rule of law, enslaved black colonials became free since Dunmore's Proclamation was a letter of patent.

Slave-owning patriots called it "conditional" and tried to discredit the proclamation. However, it was not conditional since the imperial government, through the *Declaratory Act of 1766*, had already legislatively nullified colonial slave statutes and negro laws within the American colonies. Further, England's Court of the King's Bench in the *Somerset* case struck down colonial slave statutes and laws—three years earlier in 1772. The *Somerset* decision was the law of the land within the American colonies, and Dunmore's proclamation liberated colonial blacks—the same as the colonial-born black named James Somerset and others were all liberated in 1772.

It is in the words in the proclamation where Lord Dunmore entreated "every person" ... "to resort to His Majesty's standard" and: I do hereby further declare all indentured Servants, Negroes, or others (appertaining to Rebels) free" as being a dispositive statement of the imperial government. Doubtlessly, Dunmore's proclamation, where it referenced "Negroes," in the contemplation of the English rule of law meant all people of African ancestry living within the American Colonies since slavery was never legally authorized under the English rule of law as established by England's Magna Carta of 1215, England's common law and this was reaffirmed three years earlier by the Court of the King's Bench in the *Somerset* decision in 1772.

Further, Dunmore's Proclamation in November 1775 could not be conditional under the English rule of law since the condition called "slave" did not legally exist due to England's *Magna Carta of 1215*, England's common law and Lord Mansfield's ruling three years earlier... which determined in the *Somerset* case— "slavery was not allowed and approved by the laws of this Kingdom." Moreover, the term "slave" was extralegal, and under the English rule of law, the person's race was irrelevant. Thus, Dunmore's Proclamation included all colonials, whether white or black. Furthermore, indentured servitude was recognized by the English rule of law as being the lowest social rank that existed in colonial America. Indentured servitude was the only recognized sub-category of colonial Englishman contemplated by the English rule of law—

thus, black colonials suffering as enslaved people in colonial America fell within the rubric of indentured servants, no different than which the original nineteen kidnapped Africans found themselves in 1619. The original nineteen Africans were indentured servants—not slaves.

Worried General George Washington, in his capacity as both commander-in-chief of the American Patriot forces and a concerned Virginian slave owner, expressed the sentiment that it was urgently necessary to crush Lord Dunmore's slave recruitment initiative, or the momentum of slave defection would be "like a snowball rolling" down a snow-covered hill. Dunmore's Proclamation caused Washington to believe, as he stated in a letter to Colonel Henry Lee III in December 1775, that success in the rebellion would come to whatever side could arm "Negroes" the fastest. Acting on this belief and fear, Washington reversed an earlier order, which barred all "Negroes" from enlisting in the Continental Army. Instead, changed his total prohibition upon negro recruits in the army by recruiting "free Negroes" who'd already served, as Washington worried that many of those former soldiers might cross over to the British side.

Further, Washington insisted, "I do not think that forcing his Lordship (Dunmore) on shipboard is sufficient. Nothing less than depriving him of life or liberty will secure peace to Virginia, as motives of resentment actuate his conduct to a degree equal to the total destruction of that colony." While Patriot James Madison felt that the British Southern Strategy initiative was the kind of "tampering with the slaves" that he had most feared. "To say the truth," Madison confided to a friend, "that is the only part in which this colony is vulnerable" ... "We shall fall like Achilles by the hand of one that knows that secret." However, in having been their silent partner-in-crime for over a hundred years the British knew the colony of Virginia's deep "secret." Because of this shared secret, the English called its operation "*Southern Strategy*." The British believed it would splinter the colonial coalition if they focused on the southern colonies, and it would ultimately quell rebellion throughout the American colonies.

A cohort of northern patriots believed a reconciliation with the mother country should be pursued, so Pennsylvanian patriot John Dickinson had been permitted to send an Olive Branch Petition to England's King George III in April 1775, expressing hope for reconciliation between the American Colonies and Great Britain. However, when it was reported that the King refused to read the petition—all came to believe that the relationship had been irreparably breached and that Lord Dunmore and the imperial government had the support of King George III.

The King was so displeased with his subjects in the American colonies he stated to his Ministers: "Keep the rebels harassed, anxious and poor, until the day when, by a natural and inevitable process, discontent and disappointment were converted into penitence and remorse." The British Southern Strategy forced each American patriot to view Dunmore's Proclamation personally and to realize that the Continental Congress's cohesiveness and its patriots were a "do or die" proposition.

At the Fifth Virginia Convention, held May and June 1776, the Virginian patriot and enslaver Patrick Henry made the provocative accusations that a representative of the Crown—Lord Dunmore, was "encouraging insurrection among our slaves, many of whom are now actually armed against us" ... reveals the King to be a "tyrant instead of the protector of his people." Henry's statement was not true since the condition called slavery endured by black colonials conflicted with the English rule of law. As the condition known as slavery was more described as colonial tyranny, none of those who professed ownership of black colonials truly owned them. Moreover, England's monarch and imperial government had never formally approved colonial America's hereditary slavery scheme, which made black slavery a criminal scheme that victimized His Majesty's black subjects.

It was very ironic, as the imperial government abolished all colonial slave resolutions, votes, orders, and proceedings because they questioned and violated parliamentary laws in its *Declaratory Act of 1766*, and England's highest court declared slavery was not "allowed and approved by the laws of this Kingdom" six years later in the *Somerset* decision—the imperial government and King George III were now protecting their subjects who were suffering as slaves in the American colonies. Such being the case, Henry's protestations were decrying equal protection under the rule of law for black Englishmen.

John Hancock of the colony of Massachusetts called Parliament's *Declaratory Act of 1766*— British tyranny. Pennsylvanian patriot, Dr. Benjamin Franklin framed the patriots' precarious predicament by reminding the assembled body that they "must, indeed, all hang together, or most assuredly, we shall all hang separately." Dr. Franklin's observations placed matters into perspective, as this rebellion for independence had become mortally personal for everyone.

In July 1776, America's Founding Generation created a new government—the United States of America, dedicated to the proposition that everyone would be treated the same under the rule of law. The law would be king, and this republic would be "a government of laws and not of men." But as this was the rock upon which this "more perfect union" was to be built, it necessarily meant doing away with the King at the top, born to rule, and slaves at the bottom—born to be ruled by slave masters. However, America's Founding Fathers had settled on something different—a slave nation.

The northern patriots needed the wealth of the southern planters, so it became core to this new government that slavery would be the bedrock of this developing nation's economy. And in knowing that the existence of "free negroes" would be incompatible and cancerous to this vision—they committed themselves to excluding all people of African ancestry and purging their historical contributions with repression and extreme prejudice. While all were willing to rid colonial America of the tyranny of King George III's government, northern patriots went along with southern patriots, which corrupted this nation's core founding precept—"all men are created equal" under the rule of law.

With little dispute or controversy, the coming together of the Founding Generation created an uneasy alliance of divergent ideologues, and as historian Edmund S. Morgan observed... "the men who came together to found the independent United States, dedicated to freedom and equality, either held slaves or were willing to join hands with those who did," [78] and continuing "None of them felt entirely comfortable about the fact, but neither did they feel responsible for it. Most of them had inherited both their slaves and their attachment to freedom from an earlier generation, and they knew the two were not unconnected." Further, in the book *Slave Nation: How Slavery United the Colonies and Sparked the American Revolution*, [79] the observation was made that while many patriots throughout colonial America professed to hold enmity towards black slavery on moral grounds, all capitulated to proslavery interests for the sake of unity during the American Revolutionary War era.

The *Phillipsburg Proclamation*, issued by British General Sir Henry Clinton on June 30, 1779, was an iteration of Britain's Southern Strategy. The primary purpose of this proclamation was to stimulate mass desertion by encouraging enslaved black colonials to come over to the British and pursue "any occupation which shall think proper." The offer applied to males and females, including their children, and it was estimated that 100,000 black colonials fled captivity.

The Proclamation provided as follows:

Whereas the enemy have adopted a practice of enrolling NEGROES among their Troops, I do hereby give notice That all NEGROES taken in arms, or upon any military Duty, shall be purchased for the public service at a Price; the money to be paid to the Captor.

But I do most strictly forbid any Person to sell or claim right over any NEGROE, the property of a Rebel, who may take Refuge with any part of this Army: And I do promise t every NEGROE who shall desert the Rebel standard, full security to follow within these Lines, any Occupation which he shall think proper.

Given under my Hand, at Head Quarters, PHILIPSBURG, the 30th day of June 1779. H. CLINTON

The *Phillipsburg Proclamation* reiterated and elucidated upon Dunmore's proclamation, issued in November 1775. This subsequent proclamation by the imperial government affirmed the subjecthood of black colonials suffering as slaves, as this patent of liberty was under the English rule of law. Unlike Lincoln's Emancipation Proclamation during America's Civil War—this proclamation of emancipation was wholesome and unambiguous since slavery within the American colonies was always prohibited under the English rule of law. Moreover, the imperial government legislatively nullified colonial slave statutes and negro laws by way of the *Declaratory Act of 1766*, ten years before the Declaration of Independence, and six years later, England's highest court had declared slavery was not "allowed and approved by the laws of this Kingdom." This became the law of the land in the American colonies during uncontested colonial times. It legally freed all people suffering as slaves throughout the erstwhile 13 British colonies, now American states—and it conferred liberty to 500,000 black colonials still under the English rule of law.

Further, Clinton's proclamation aligned with the Crown's duty to protect its subjects under the colonial charter, and as Parliament had legislatively abolished colonial slave statutes and laws under the *Declaratory Act of 1766* and slavery was declared unconstitutional by the Court of the King's Bench in the *Somerset* case, none needed to escape captivity or put themselves in mortal jeopardy to claim liberty under the *Magna Carta* and the *English Bill of Rights of 1689*.

In part, America's disinformation campaign regarding Dunmore's Proclamation, the haplessness and illiteracy of the black Englishmen, and Clinton's belief that an unconditional grant of liberty for all colonial blacks would turn the lagging war around drove the decision to issue this proclamation. Militarily, Clinton thought—if successful, countless black Englishmen would flee from their masters—striking a blow at the southern plantation economy and would force southern slave masters to use their men for guarding slaves instead of fighting them.

After issuing the *Phillipsburg Proclamation*, General Clinton headed south to South Carolina, where he made impressive inroads. Although some South Carolina Patriots like John Laurens had tried to convince the rebel government to free and arm slaves to swell the ranks of the otherwise rag-tagged American troops, the economic and social structure was too entrenched. Laurens even argued that by sending slaves into military service, insurrections at home would be less likely, but his argument ultimately failed. Charleston fell to the British, in part because Black pilots helped the British navy navigate the waters around the city. When the British captured him with the fall of Charleston, Laurens blamed the Patriots' failure to use Black soldiers for the loss. His compatriots, deeply committed to upholding a slave society even as they fought for "freedom' from 'slavery' by the British, offered Loyalist slaves as rewards or in lieu of payment to Patriot soldiers.

Clinton remained in command of the British Army in North America until after the Battle of Yorktown, where his subordinate General Cornwallis surrendered on October 19, 1781. It was one of the last major land battles in North America. In the summer of 1782, Clinton gave up his post. He returned to England, replaced by Sir Guy Carleton, who oversaw the cessation of hostilities and coordinated the evacuation of British troops in 1783.

VII. THE TREATY OF PARIS OF 1783

By early 1782, France, an ally of the developing nation America, had withdrawn her military forces. Various state governments were swamped with remonstrance and petitions that especially complained of the war's burdens on ordinary Americans. Additionally, many petitions charged wealthy Americans with armchair patriotism, evidenced by their reluctance to take the battlefield and the fact that the rich were not taking equal responsibility in the war effort. Further, there were supply problems, and the value of the Continental paper dollar was plummeting, which served to pay America's soldiers and caused a mutiny. This pay-focused uprising framed America's principal wartime mobilization challenge—economics. Thus, the United States sued for peace and chose Benjamin Franklin, John Jay, John Adams, Thomas Jefferson, and Henry Laurens to negotiate the terms on behalf of the United States in Paris, France.

During the negotiations, everyone recognized that the plight of the 500,000 black colonials was a hurdle to finalizing a peace treaty. This was because the British were reticent on the issues of honoring its rule of law and Clinton's *Phillipsburg Proclamation*, which announced liberty rights to all enslaved people in colonial America. However, terms for cessation of hostilities were finally agreed to, and the *Treaty of Paris of 1783* was signed by all peace negotiators—except Thomas Jefferson.

Many historians have observed that by envisioning the U.S. as a future major trading partner, the British imperial government had a statesmanlike perspective in finalizing the *Treaty of Paris* and made the treaty terms extremely favorable to the U.S. However, it became apparent that despite England's affability, cordiality, and favorable terms, Congress could not guarantee that its citizens would adhere to the treaty's terms.

Further, once news of a treaty to cease hostilities with England was known, America's founding generation began attacking and kidnapping Blacks with impunity. Freemen and former slaves were kidnapped off public streets—in their homes and summarily placed into slavery. None of the Blacks were conferred due process of law, and the government of the United States did nothing to enforce the rule of law or to honor the terms of the international treaty. The actions of the Americans were brutal, audacious, and widespread, breaking the cessation of the hostility truce between Great Britain and the United States.

A Black loyalist named Boston King summarized the times thusly:

"The horrors and devastation of war was happily terminated, and peace was restored between America and Great Britain, which diffused universal joy among all parties except us, who had escaped from slavery and taken refuge in the English army, for a report prevailed at New York, that all the slaves, in number 2,000 were to be delivered up to their masters altho' some of them had been three or four years among the English. This dreadful rumour filled us all with inexpressible anguish and terror, especially when we saw our old masters coming from Virginia, North Carolina, and other parts and seizing upon their slaves in the streets of New York; or even dragging them out of their beds. Many of the slaves had very cruel masters so that the thoughts of returning home with them embittered life to us."

Reacting to these events in May 1783, British General Guy Carleton, Commander-in-Chief, complained to an American delegation that included General George Washington, labeling the Americans' actions concerning Black colonials as renewed "hostilities." Carleton informed Washington that it was the official position of the British imperial government that all former slaves were free British subjects and were not property under the English rule of law adopted by the United States. The enslaver Washington disagreed, responding that all former slaves were "property" owned by citizens of the United States based upon colonial slave statutes and laws, and in being "property," he requested their surrender, control, and custody. This claim made no sense since Parliament abolished colonial slave statutes and laws in section II of the *Declaratory Act of 1766*. Lord Chief Justice Mansfield of the Court of the King's

Bench also struck down colonial statutes and laws in the 1772 *Somerset* case.

The British General Carleton refused, stating that these people were free Englishmen under the rule of law, not chattel property, following Clinton's *Phillipsburg Proclamation* in 1779. "The clear import of treaty language controls unless application of the words of the treaty according to their meaning affects a result inconsistent with the intent or experiences of its signatories." *Sumitomo Shoji Amer., Inc. v. Avagliano*, 457 U. S. 176, 180 (1982).

This framed a pivotal legal issue that Taney, in the *Dred Scott* decision, should have been conscientiously addressed, as Carleton argued that people granted freedom before the treaty could not be considered property as a matter of English law.

General Carleton stated to Washington that he did not see any provision in the *Articles of Peace* as a relinquishment or an abandonment of the imperial government's grant of liberation of the colonial slave population. He went on to explain, to General Washington's dismay and chagrin, that it would be a breach of faith and honor for him not to abide by Clinton's *Phillipsburg Proclamation* or the English rule of law that established the ethnicity of the 500,000 black colonials held in captivity by the Americans as Englishmen and his countrymen—entitled to his protection in being the King's subjects. Carleton stated he planned to remove all Revolutionary War-era blacks from the United States when he left America.

However, tension de-escalated when Carleton suggested that this matter be resolved by their sovereigns and, on behalf of England, pledged compensation from the British government if removing these people was deemed a treaty violation. To provide for that possibility, both he and Washington agreed to generate separate registries, called the *Book of Negroes,* listing their names, ages, and occupations, along with the names of their former masters, so that "the owners might eventually be paid for the slaves who were not entitled to their freedom by British Proclamation and promises." Carleton and Washington each kept an accounting of those removed from the United States. The British only evacuated 3,000 people from the United States, and Americans detained 500,000 black Englishmen.

After the *Treaty of Paris of 1783* ended the American Revolution—500,000 black Englishmen found themselves in legal limbo and denied liberty here in the United States. Further, they were entitled to due process of law, which was denied to them, and they became the bedrock of America's slave-based economy before the ratification of America's Constitution in the late 1780s.

The delegates to the constitutional convention during the late 1780s were aware of the unresolved state of this matter. However, the Constitution, led by Virginian James Madison, hailed the "Father of the

Constitution," ratified the Three-Fifths Clause, which states that an enslaved person counts as "three-fifths" of a person for the purpose of apportioning congressional representatives and taxes, and the fugitive-slave clause, which commands that an enslaved person... "escaping into another" state, regardless of its laws, "shall be delivered" back to the slave owner.

The fact that colonial slavery was a criminal scheme and colonial slave statutes and laws were legislatively nullified by the *Declaratory Act of* 1766—ruled unconstitutional by England's highest court in the *Somerset* case in 1772—also, black colonials being emancipated by the British imperial government during colonial times—and 500,000 black Englishmen being denied the fundamental right to due process of law, are all inconvenient truths and, in consequence, slavery was not legally imported into America, and America's Constitution is not a "color-blind" document.

VIII. THE CONSTITUTION REVEALED

The U.S. Supreme Court in *Dred Scott*, while stating that it analyzed colonial slave and negro laws in the American colonies, ignored and did not consider England's *Declaratory Act* which abolished hereditary slave resolutions and slavery laws in 1766. Moreover, Taney professed that black Englishmen were slaves when the U.S. declared independence from Britain in 1776; instead, they were free black Englishmen suffering under colonial governmental tyranny in violation of the

English rule of law. Singularly, this was a significant misapprehension of the history of colonial slavery.

Equally perplexing—Taney, in the *Dred Scott* case, ignored hereditary slavery's violation of parliamentary laws and gave no account to Parliament's *Declaratory Act of 1766,* which abolished "all resolutions, votes, orders, and proceedings," such as Virginia's resolution *partus sequitur ventrem* in 1662 and Virginia's Slave Laws of 1705 since they questioned Parliament's power and authority to enact binding colonial laws. These repugnant colonial resolutions became endemic throughout the American colonies, although they violated parliamentary laws. Nor did America's high court give any heed to the *Somerset* decision, which was decided in 1772—three years before the "shot heard around the world" was fired in Concord that slavery was "odious" and not "allowed and approved by the laws of this Kingdom."

Principally, when the thirteen colonies declared independence from Britain, the black population of 500,000 were legally free British citizens under the English rule of law since most were born slaves under hereditary slave resolutions and negro laws enacted by colonial assemblies, which were rendered "utterly null and void." These hereditary slave resolutions, votes, orders, and proceedings were declared "null and void" ten years earlier under the *Declaratory Act*.

Thomas Jefferson recognized the constitutional problems laid bare in the *Somerset* decision and strongly advocated for a clean break from the mother country—Great Britain. After the Declaration of Independence in July 1776—Jefferson and other slave-holding Founding Fathers immediately moved the U.S. Congress to supplant Anglo-Saxon jurisprudence and the English common law for Roman law.

Jefferson and his allies were unsuccessful as the U.S. Congress rejected Jefferson's motion and formally adopted Anglo-Saxon jurisprudence and the English common law as America's rule of law in July 1776. This contentious discussion regarding the abandonment of the English rule of law and numerous last-minute edits to the grievance section of the Declaration of Independence by his zealously proslavery colleagues, where Jefferson blamed the King for fastening black bondage upon the unwilling white colonists, created tension, resentment, and mistrust.

Jefferson had concluded the grievance section of the Declaration by accusing the King of:

"... exciting those very people to rise in arms among us, and to purchase that liberty of which he has deprived them, by murdering the people on whom he has obtruded them; thus paying of former crimes committed against the Liberties of one people, with crimes which he urges them to commit against the lives of another."

Along with its gross-deception, Jefferson's indictment against King George III documents his fearful concerns over the imperial government's legislative, judicial, and executive actions during colonial times and their applicability to his own Virginia plantation. Due to its historic nature and the full-throated discussion attenuated to Jefferson's Roman law motion, the Declaration of Independence caused Benjamin Franklin to warn the members of the U.S. Congress again— "We must all hang together; or most assuredly, we shall all hang separately." While John Adams, for his part, observed, "...facts are stubborn things; and whatever may be our wishes, our inclinations, or the dictates of our passion, they cannot alter the state of facts and evidence."

Significantly, the Framers of America's Constitution ignored the fundamental Anglo-Saxon jurisprudential doctrine of due process and the rule of law when they ratified the Constitution in the 1780s. Among various shortcomings, the Framers ignored that the United States did not afford black Englishmen the fundamental right to due process of law before their liberty was taken from them. Due process of law was authorized under America's rule of law. Moreover, black colonials had credible legal arguments in support of the claim for liberty, and they were summarily and improperly institutionalized. This caused 500,000 black colonials to become "slaves" in derogation of the controlling rule of law. The Framers of America's Constitution caused a class of colonial Englishmen to be recognized as "three-fifths" a person for representation—all were of African descent.

The adoption of Anglo-Saxon jurisprudence by the U.S. Congress over Jefferson's strident objections, as well as each of the thirteen state governments' adoption of Anglo-Saxon jurisprudence in 1776... fastened the U.S. and the Framers of the Constitution during the ratification process during the 1780s to Anglo-Saxon jurisprudential doctrines of due process under law, *jus soli,* and the English common law. America's adoption of the English rule of law foreclosed and prohibited all property ownership claims of America's Founding Generation concerning Revolutionary War-era black colonials and does eviscerate the talking point of originalists that America ratified a "color-blind" constitution during the 1780s as it denied due process to colonial-born blacks and sanctioned the enslavement of 500,000 black Englishmen.

Until the new Constitution was ratified, the Articles of Confederation governed the country. That document was tailored to a newly formed nation, made the states act more like independent, sovereign countries, and it quickly became clear to some of America's leaders that future stability required a stronger, more centralized government. New York's Alexander Hamilton thus led the call for a constitutional convention to reevaluate the nation's governing document.

The initial purpose of the Convention was for the delegates to amend the Articles of Confederation; however, the ultimate outcome was the proposal and creation of a completely new form of government. Three months later, on September 17, 1787, the Convention concluded with the signing (by 38 out of 41 delegates present) of the new U.S. Constitution. Under Article VII, it was agreed that the document would not be binding until nine of the 13 existing states ratified it.

The question of ratification—citizens quickly separated into two groups: Federalists and Anti-Federalists. The Federalists supported it. They tended to be among the elite members of society—wealthy and well-educated landowners, businessmen, and former military commanders who believed a strong government would be better for national defense and economic growth. Hamilton and Virginian James Madison led the lobbying efforts for votes to ratify the Constitution. With assistance from John Jay, they produced 85 essays known as "The Federalist Papers" that explained and defended how the proposed new government would function. The essays were published in newspapers nationwide.

On June 21, 1788, the Constitution became the official framework of the government of the United States of America when New Hampshire became the ninth of the 13 states to ratify it. The ratification process was long, contentious, and "color-conscious." For example, Article 1, Section 9, Clause 1 is one of a handful of provisions in the original Constitution related to black slavery; though it does not use the word "slave," it was known as *"The Slave Trade Clause."*

This Clause prohibited the federal government from limiting the importation of "person," understood to mean enslaved people of African ancestry, where the existing state governments saw fit to allow, until twenty years after the Constitution took effect. It was a compromise between the Southern States, where slavery was pivotal to the economy, and states where the abolition of slavery had been accomplished or was contemplated.

Further, the apportionment in the House of Representatives and the number of electoral votes each State would have in presidential elections based on a State's population was quite thorny. The Southern States wanted to count the entire slave population. This would increase the number of members of Congress. The Northern delegates and others who opposed slavery wished to count only free persons, including free blacks in the North and South. This dispute was resolved by compromise with the Three-Fifths Clause, which states that an enslaved person counts as "three-fifths" of a person to apportion congressional representatives and taxes.

In 1793, Congress passed the first of two federal statutes that allowed for the capture and return of runaway enslaved people within the territory of the United States called the *Fugitive Slave Act,* which authorized local government to seize and return escapees to their owners and imposed penalties on anyone who aided in their flight. Widespread resistance to the 1793 law led to the passage of the *Fugitive Slave Act of 1850*, which added more provisions regarding runaways and levied harsher penalties for interfering in their capture.

The Supreme Court "functions as guardian and interpreter of the Constitution." However, the law is King—not men in the United States. In *Smith v. Browe & Cooper*, Chief Justice Holt ruled that "As soon as a negro comes to England he is free; one may be a *villien* in England, but not a slave," and Lord Chief Justice Mansfield in the *Somerset* case, [80] that ruled slavery was not "allowed and approved by the laws of this Kingdom." [81] And while the English common law provided— "no man can have a property [interest] in another" ... "being black did not prove the property," [82] and the law took "no notice of negroes being different from other men," [83] this "color-conscious" constitution egged on America's polarization of the questions of slavery, disharmony, and sectionalism—hurling the country towards civil war. In failing to guarantee black colonials' due process rights, as provided for under the rule of law—the U.S. Constitution ratified their unlawful enslavement and exploitation under the guise of the rule of law. America's white slaveholders should have been required to prove their ownership claims of the 500,000 black Englishmen.

Thomas Jefferson knew that America's law needed to be true, or none of it could withstand historical reflection or analysis. Such was the reason Jefferson advocated for the supplantation of the English rule of law in July 1776. Jefferson advocated for a clean break away from Anglo-Saxon jurisprudential doctrine and the adoption of Roman Law, perhaps recognizing that this would offer the U.S. a creditable legal basis to whitewash the criminal origins of black slavery. Or maybe Jefferson was a visionary being who knew that any putative claim of ownership of another person needed to be grounded in a written law.

Jefferson, a well-versed and learned lawyer, was, arguably highly apprehensive about the legal status and plight of colonial American blacks as Virginia's hereditary slavery resolution of *partus sequitur ventrem* and related proceedings—had been declared "utterly null and void" in section II of the *Declaratory Act of 1766* when he delivered his final draft of the Declaration of Independence to the Committee of the whole in early July 1776. Jefferson wanted to abandon the English rule of law as he recognized and understood the power, authority, and scope of the doctrine of parliamentary sovereignty.

Jefferson understood that Lord Chief Justice Mansfield of the Court of the King's Bench in the *Somerset* case had also struck down all colonial slave statutes and laws and ruled that slavery was not "allowed and approved by the laws of this Kingdom." Since a sole house of a colonial legislature could not credibly claim that it had proclaimed hereditary slavery was a lawful condition—he saw only one course of action. Jefferson was grappling with the reality of his situation and other enslavers—when he began to advocate the supplementation of the English rule of law for Roman Law.

Moreover, he probably thought of Enlightenment philosophers like John Locke or Charles-Louis Secondat, Baron de Montesquieu's observation that "the misfortune of a republic... happens when the people are gained by bribery and corruption; in this case, they grow indifferent to public affairs, and avarice becomes their primary passion." Thus, Jefferson advocated that this developing nation adopt Roman Law and break historical ties with Anglo-Saxon jurisprudential doctrines and the English common law. However, the U.S. Congress was unpersuaded.

The U.S. Congress formally adopted Anglo-Saxon jurisprudence and the English rule of law in July 1776. Further, each of the thirteen states followed suit—enacting reception statutes adopting Anglo-Saxon jurisprudence and the English rule of law. Thus, with the U.S. Congress and each state government adopting the English rule of law, the Nation and the states were legally obligated to afford all black colonials a habeas corpus hearing *before* depriving them of liberty—which did not occur. The refusal to grant black colonials a due process hearing implicated the ratification process of the U.S. Constitution—as the wholesale failure to confer upon the 500,000 black colonials a due process hearing has significant implications. This is because the U.S. Congress adopted the English rule of law. England's *Magna Carta of 1215* guaranteed a due process hearing to everyone in the realm and other Anglo-Saxon jurisprudential doctrines—the law of this land.

Yet, Chief Justice Taney ruled in the *Dred Scott* case that all people of African ancestry, whether enslaved or free, were not citizens of the United States and, therefore, did not have the right to sue in federal court. This could have been a reasonable legal conclusion, with no inference of race consciousness—if the 13 state governments had granted the 500,000 black Englishmen a habeas corpus hearing *before* the Constitution was ratified. This did not occur.

Moreover, Taney's race consciousness becomes more apparent with his finding that, at the time of the ratification of the U.S. Constitution, persons of African descent were brought to the U.S. as property and, whether later freed or not, could not become U.S. citizens. Taney's statement was pure misdirection since black colonials were not conferred the fundamental right to a due process hearing—a right to which the rule of law authorized and was mandated, without regard for the merits of their portended claims. Also, Taney's findings were false, as the black colonials were born in colonial America and, by virtue of their birth in the American colonies, were Englishmen. Additionally, the first nineteen kidnapped Africans that arrived on the shores of the colony of Virginia in 1619 were indentured servants—not slaves, and the English rule of law authorized their legal status. After indentured servitude, they became British subjects under the English rule of law.

Jefferson wrote in 1823, reflecting upon his penning the Declaration of Independence and stating that other members of the Committee "unanimously pressed on myself alone to undertake the draught [sic]. I consented; I drew it; but before I reported it to the committee I communicated it separately to Dr. Franklin and Mr. Adams requesting their corrections. I then wrote a fair copy, reported it to the committee and from the unaltered to the Congress." Jefferson forever complained that the subsequent actions of Congress "mangled" the Declaration of Independence since it refused his plea for the supplantation of the English rule of law, presumably due to hereditary slavery criminal origins and the subsequent legislation and judicial actions of the imperial government.

In the *Dred Scott* decision, the Supreme Court distinguished state citizenship from federal citizenship and found the latter precluded to African Americans because of whom the Court believed the founders meant to exclude in the original Constitution. Taney concluded that Native Americans, on the other hand, were considered free and independent residents of North America at the time of the founding, so they could become federal citizens of the United States. This legal reasoning barred Dred Scott, an African American—and Taney found that he could not sue for his freedom from his time spent in the (at the time) federal territory of Wisconsin because, as the Court interpreted the Constitution, African Americans could not become federal citizens.

Whether the Framers ratified a "color blind" U.S. Constitution must be viewed and analyzed through the prism of the *Dred Scott* decision, Anglo-Saxon jurisprudence, and the English rule of law *circa* 1787. Thusly, and destructive to the viability of originalism as championed by conservatives is the fact that all pretended colonial slave statutes and laws were the product of a criminal scheme initiated and masterminded by corrupt colonial assemblymen who conspired with others to purport to enact valid slave statutes and negro laws authorizing slavery at birth for people of African descent living in the American colonies during the 1660s. Under the English rule of law, slavery in colonial America could only be approved and authorized by a "positive law," a legislative power vested only with the Parliament of Great Britain, which it had not exercised.

The Parliament of Great Britain, under its *Declaratory Act of 1766*, exercised parliamentary sovereignty and legislatively "abolished" all pretended slave statutes and negro laws enacted by colonial assemblies within the American colonies that lacked the approval of the imperial government or England's King by declaring such instruments "utterly null and void" in 1766. The colonial assemblymen within the American colonies breached the colonial charter. They criminally violated the *Sedition Act of 1661* by enacting laws without securing the approval of England's King or the imperial government.

The liberty rights of all colonial blacks who suffered as enslaved people in the American colonies were restored to the status quo under the English rule of law. Further, it is significant to note that in responding to the *Declaratory Act of 1766*, memorialized in the Declaration of Independence—America's Founding Generation came to indict England's King George III and his imperial government in the grievance section of that document for that legislative act, and as being a tyrant for among other things... *"For taking away our Charters, abolishing our most valuable laws, and altering fundamentally the Forms of our Governments,"* and *"For suspending our own Legislatures, and declaring themselves invested with power to legislate for us in all cases whatsoever"*—language specially taken out of the *Declaratory Act of 1766*.

The legal nullification of the hub-and-spoke conspiracy called hereditary slavery before the Declaration of Independence in July 1776 undermines the claim that the U.S. Constitution's ratification process was "color-blind." The hereditary slavery scheme violated each colonial charter and Parliament's *Sedition Act of 1661,* which mandated the imperial government's assent, which included England's King upon all colonial statutes, resolutions, orders, votes, proceedings, and laws. Corrupt colonial assemblymen, in league with colonial governors, did not secure the assent of the imperial government upon portended colonial legislation and, by so doing, intruded upon the exclusive power and authority of the Parliament to make statutes and laws throughout the Kingdom of Great Britain. Being advised, Parliament's *Declaratory Act of 1766* abolished all pretended colonial slave statutes and negro laws for want of jurisdiction to enact a "positive law" throughout the American colonies.

Moreover, the Court of the King's Bench in the *Somerset* decision affirmed parliamentary sovereignty—struck down colonial slave practices and pretended slave laws in June 1772—restoring liberty rights and privileges to all colonial blacks suffering as slaves within the American colonies, as a matter of the English rule of law. The criminal origins of hereditary slavery during the 1660s—Parliament abolishment of colonial "resolutions, votes, orders, and Proceedings" in 1766 and its legal nullification before the Declaration of Independence controlled the legal question of whether white Americans owned black colonials before the Declaration of Independence and directly impacted the threshold question of whether a "color-blind" U.S. Constitution was ratified during the 1780s.

The decision of the Framers of the Constitution to ignore the English rule of law's fundamental protection of due process of law caused the unceremonious and unlawful enslavement of 500,000 colonial blacks after the *Treaty of Paris of 1783*. The Framers of the Constitution were bound by the English rule of law, which mandated the due process of law for everyone. The denial of due process to the 500,000 black colonials during the early 1780s and the *Dred Scott* decision prevented even the suggestion that the ratification of the U.S. Constitution was "color-blind."

Additionally, as the Supreme Court in the *Dred Scott* decision is controlling precedent on the question of a "color-blind" constitution, and as Taney stated, "… the legislation and histories of the times, and the language used in the Declaration of Independence, show, that neither the class of persons who had been imported as slaves, nor their descendants, whether they had become free or not, were then acknowledged as a part of the people, nor intended to be included in the general words used in that memorable instrument."

However, Taney's declarant is contradicted and disproven by the status and treatment accorded to the original nineteen kidnapped Africans who arrived in the colony of Virginia in 1619. They were indentured servants—not slaves. Moreover, after their terms were completed, these Africans, no different from white immigrants, became British subjects when they completed their indenture term. They were then eligible for headrights for land in this new British colony in the Chesapeake Bay region, where former indentured servants settled and were common.

Further, the children of the original Africans, born in colonial Virginia, were born free British subjects. For example, an original African named Anthony Johnson, whose indenture ended in 1635. Afterward, Johnson married an African woman named Mary, and he and she had three children who were free-born Englishmen. Further, the colony of Virginia officials exempted his wife and two daughters from paying taxes "during their natural lives."

Elizabeth Key's mother was also an original African; her father was a white colonial Englishman. She was an "illegitimate child" born in 1630 in the colony of Virginia and placed in indentured servitude. Her indenture was transferred to a justice of the peace named John Mottram. In 1650, Mottram paid for the passage of several young English indentured servants. One of them was William Grinstead. Elizabeth and William soon began a relationship and had a son named John. John Mottram died in 1655, and his heirs designated Key as enslaved—not indentured and asserted that she and her son belonged to Mottram's estate. William Grinstead, now free from his indenture and practicing law, represented Key and their son as they sued for freedom from the Mottram's in court.

Key's case hinged on several legal arguments. Firstly, was the fact that her father, Thomas Key, was English and that according to the English rule of law— one's legal status as free or in bondage followed that of the father. Secondly, she had been in indentured servitude for ten years longer than she should have: Thomas Key had stipulated that she was to be set free when she was fifteen. Finally, she argued that she had been baptized as a child and was a practicing Christian, and should not be enslaved. She lost her case in appeals court but petitioned the General Assembly to investigate her case. A committee was formed to investigate, and they sided with Elizabeth, determining that she was free based on her father's status and baptism.

The treatment of these colonial-born Englishmen during the 1650s established equal social and political relations, making Johnson and Key's significant black colonials as they symbolize a routine social status and ranking of people of African ancestry—a status and hierarchy that was practically and theoretically incompatible with a system of racial repression.

CONCLUSION

The *Dred Scott* decision is the law of the land, and it conclusively resolves the routinely mentioned talking point of originalists, strict constructionists, and conservative jurists who claim that America's Constitution is color-blind. This decision of the Supreme Court stands inapposite to this repeated claim of originalists, and the *Dred Scott* decision's durability and long-standing status as the law of the land here in America goes to the heart of whether a "color-blind" constitution is operative in this nation. The *Dred Scott* decision is probative—and conclusive—since this Supreme Court decision has been the law of the land for 168 years.

Further, a Virginian drafted the Declaration of Independence. Another Virginian led the Colonies to victory over British oppression. Another Virginian drafted the Constitution and the Bill of Rights. Another Virginian was then installed as the Chief Justice of the U.S. Supreme Court. For the first thirty-six years of our Country's existence, the Presidency would be occupied by Virginians for thirty-two of those years. All these persons were dynastic slaveholders from the colony of Virginia. Indeed, all knew that their independence and subjugation of 500,000 black colonials was historically foul—as slavery within the American colonies was an extralegal institution, the handiwork of Virginia's *House of Burgesses*, its Virginian conspirators and as Virginian families such as theirs had profited from this misanthrope, criminal, and corrupt scheme—that their wealth, families legacies, and their own had become inextricably linked and interwoven to the sustainability of a mythical and a noble emergence of the United States.

Moreover, the former white colonials who claimed ownership of these black people after the U.S. Congress ratified the *Treaty of Paris of 1783* in January 1784 were still legally and morally obligated to prove their alleged legal ownership claims under the English rule of law, adopted by the U.S. Congress over Thomas Jefferson's strident opposition in July 1776. They did not do so, and if they had adhered to the English rule of law or international traditions—it would have led to freedom for the 500,000 black colonials, as colonial slavery was a criminal condition within the American colonies when the 13 British colonies declared themselves a new nation of people in July 1776. The rule of English law established by the *Somerset* decision in 1772 meant liberty for the 500,000 black colonials, and they knew it.

In June of 1772, Lord Chief Justice Mansfield delivered the opinion of the Court of the King's Bench. The trial was a judicial review of American slave laws conducted by Mansfield. Still, the *Somerset* opinion carried the concurrence of the other eleven judges temporarily elevated to the Court of the King's Bench.

> "The state of slavery is of such a nature, that it is incapable of being introduced on any reasons, moral or political; but only positive law, which preserves its force long after the reasons, occasion, and the time itself from whence it was created, is erased from memory; it's so odious, that nothing can be suffered to support it, but positive law."

The U.S. Congress's adoption of Anglo-Saxon jurisprudence and England's common law in July 1776 created an insurmountable problem for U.S. constitutionalism as declared American slaves laws were not "positive law." That slavery was not "allowed and approved by the laws of this Kingdom." Further, only the Parliament of Great Britain could enact a positive law during colonial times, and even if colonial slave laws had not been declared unconstitutional, colonial slave laws were not countersigned and approved by England's King per each colonial charter. Moreover, Parliament abolished such repugnant slave laws since they violated parliamentary laws under the *Declaratory Act of 1766.*

From its ratification—the U.S. Constitution was overtly race-conscious as it relates to black Americans, and the Supreme Court's 1857 *Dred Scott* decision approved and validated a color-conscious constitution that ratified the denial of fundamental due process rights to 500,000 black Englishmen in America after the Revolution ended in 1783. The Supreme Court's decision in *Dred Scott* ignored colonial slavery's lawless origin and the significance of the Founding Fathers' indictment of the imperial government and King George III's alleged transgressions against the Founding Generation for "*abolishing our most valuable laws and altering fundamentally the Forms of our Governments,*" which were grieved and prominently declared in the grievance section of the Declaration of Independence.

Moreover, Taney's opinion revised British colonial history to create a racial order of white supremacy upon the emergence of the United States of America in 1776—ignored England's common law that prohibited slavery on sovereign soil—colonial charters binding colonial assemblies to the English rule of law and necessarily gave no attention to the *Declaratory Act of 1766* or the *Somerset* decision in 1772 to legitimize the summary enslavement of 500,000 black Englishmen in violation of the U.S. rule of law after the U.S. Congress ratified the *Treaty of Paris of 1783* authorizing that they should be "set at liberty " which officially ended the Revolution to legitimize U.S. slavery; abolished during colonial times. Due to a weak and ineffectual *Articles of Confederation of 1777*, America's first Constitution—black Englishmen were not given due process of law and were placed below the rule of law, which the Framers of the U.S. Constitution who profited from the misanthrope practice of slavery benefitted.

Led by Congressman Thaddeus Stevens, the *Radical Republicans* in the U.S. Congress were committed to the immediate and permanent end to slavery within the United States by enacting the 13th, 14th, and 15th Amendments, also known as the *Reconstruction* Amendments during the mid-1860s. These Amendments to the U.S. Constitution were color-conscious.

The congressional legislation embodied in the 13th, 14th, and 15th Amendments were not color-blind, as it was envisioned and designed to treat the black race differently—to grant black Americans rights to counter-act the misanthrope practice of enslaving people at birth in the United States and be consistent with the U.S. Constitution. Firstly, the 13th Amendment freed black slaves—but its scope was disputed before it even went into effect. Secondly, the *Radical Republicans*, the Framers, then enacted the 14th Amendment to enshrine principles outlined in the 13th Amendment in the Constitution to protect the new *Civil Rights Act* from being declared unconstitutional by the Supreme Court and thirdly, to prevent a future Congress from altering this Act by a mere majority vote. [84]

Additionally, the legislative history of the 14th Amendment establishes that it was also responding to violence against black people within the Southern States. The Congress's *Joint Committee on Reconstruction* found that only a Constitutional amendment could protect black people's rights and welfare within these states. The U.S. Supreme Court stated in *Shelley v.*

Kraemer, 334 U.S. 1 (1948) that the historical context leading to the Fourteenth Amendment's adoption must be taken into account and that this historical context reveals the Amendment's fundamental purpose and that the provisions of the Amendment are to be construed in light of this fundamental purpose.

Further, the Supreme Court in *Shelley* stated: "The historical context in which the Fourteenth Amendment became a part of the Constitution should not be forgotten. Whatever else the framers sought to achieve, it is clear that the matter of primary concern was the establishment of equality in the enjoyment of basic civil and political rights and the preservation of those rights from discriminatory action on the part of the States based on consideration of race or color" [...] "The provisions of the Amendments are to be construed in light of this fundamental purpose." *Shelley,* U.S. 334 at 23.

Sadly, as this nation underwent a massive civil rights transformation from the end of the Civil War to now, color-blind constitutionalism evolved from an argument made by Radical Republicans to one championed by racial conservatives. What was once a legal framework for justifying the extension of citizenship and rights to oppressed black Americans (criminally enslaved) is now an argument for the unconstitutionality of any measure intended to address the harms caused by the state-sanctioned denial of those rights. In its application today, color-blind means protecting white Americans from the discrimination that some conservatives perceive results from attempts to remediate historical wrongs.

The U.S. Supreme Court in *Dred Scott* did not suddenly imagine that Blacks had no rights that white men were bound to respect. This notion bridges back to colonial times, and it is clear that the Framers of the U.S. Constitution, led by the Virginian enslaver James Madison, hailed as the "Father of the Constitution," was a true believer and a devotee of this vile notion of white supremacy who saw color first as 500,000 black Englishmen were denied fundamental due process of law—claimed as slaves by Madison and his cohort and summarily made the bedrock of America's slave-based economy.

The *Dred Scott* decision and its status as the law of the land reflect our national identity as the origin story of U.S. constitutionalism—it is a tale of systemic colonial government corruption, tyranny, and countless misanthropic actions after the *Treaty of Paris of 1783* was ratified by the U.S. Congress in January 1784. Further, without regard to the rule of law, black Englishmen were declared by legal fiat as lesser human beings of a lesser order in a hyper "color-conscious" legal decision that has been denounced for its overt racism—perceived judicial activism—and poor legal reasoning. [85] And while after the Civil War—the U.S. Congress enacted the 13th Amendment in 1865, the 14th Amendment in 1868, and the 15th Amendment in 1870, it is still an overwhelmingly significant fact that the *Dred Scott* decision remained the law of the land and was strengthened in 1873 by the Supreme Court's rulings in the *Slaughterhouse Cases. Dred Scott*—is still the law of the land.

Hereditary slavery resulted from a criminal conspiracy based upon unlawful colonial legislative fiats, which became endemic throughout the American colonies. However, the British imperial government abolished all pretended colonial legislative proceedings and resolutions in 1766. Further, England's highest court struck down colonial slave statutes and laws six years later with the *Somerset* decision, which affirmed parliamentary sovereignty over lesser and inferior legislative bodies within the American colonies and ruled that slavery was not "allowed and approved by the laws of this Kingdom" in 1772. This judicial determination abolished and nullified all colonial slave fiats "for all purposes whatsoever."

In contrast, the Founding Fathers heard delegate Thomas Jefferson's detailed arguments asking the U.S. Congress to supplant Anglo-Saxon jurisprudence for Roman law, which were conscientiously considered and rejected by Congress's formal adoption of the English rule of law over Jefferson's strident objections after the 13 colonies declared independence from Great Britain. The Congress of the United States fastened this new nation to controlling Anglo-Saxon jurisprudential doctrines of due process of law and England's common liberty rights for all people born within the realm in July 1776: no Englishman could be born a slave.

Without regard to being a nation of laws, not men, originalists and conservatives hold the U.S. Constitution ratified in 1789 as a hallowed document—that must be applied and relegates its statutory construction and interpretation to the Framers and how ordinary people understood it in the late 1780s. This is a problematic and counter-intuitive approach, as it encourages everyone to ignore the Declaration of Independence—Congress's thoughtful adoption of the English rule of law in 1776 and the *Articles of Confederation*, America's first U.S. Constitution in 1777. Thus, the U.S. Constitution must be interpreted through the English rule of law, as adopted by Congress in 1776, and the *Articles of Confederation of 1777*—not just the Framers and how ordinary people understood the Constitution.

The day after appointing a committee to write the Declaration of Independence, the Second Continental Congress named another committee to write the *Articles of Confederation*. The members worked from June 1776 until November 1777, when they sent a draft to the states for ratification. On December 16, 1777, Virginia became the first state to ratify the *Articles of Confederation*, and Maryland was the last, withholding ratification until March 1, 1781.

The *Articles of Confederation* served as the written document that established the functions of the national government of the United States after it declared independence from Great Britain. It gave the U.S. Congress the power and authority to make war and to declare peace, negotiate diplomatic and commercial agreements with foreign countries, and resolve disputes between the States. However, under the *Articles*—Congress had no actual power to enforce its requests to the states—for troops—for money—to pay the nation's debts—or to honor the terms of its treaties with Great Britain or Native American nations. By the end of 1786, the *Shays' Rebellion*, which highlighted federal governmental ineffectiveness and the shortcomings of the *Articles of Confederation,* led to a push for a constitutional convention, evolving into a new U.S. constitution in 1789. [86]

The *Articles of Confederation* established a sovereign, national government and, as such, limited the rights of the states to conduct their own diplomacy and foreign policy. However, this proved difficult to enforce, as the weak national government could not prevent the state of Georgia from pursuing its own independent policy regarding Spanish Florida, attempting to occupy disputed territories and threatening war if Spanish officials did not work to curb Native American attacks or refrain from harboring escaped black colonials. Nor could the national government prevent the landing of convicts that the British Government continued to export to its former colonies.

Further, the *Articles of Confederation* did not allow Congress sufficient authority to enforce provisions of the *Treaty of Paris of 1783* concerning the 500,000 black Englishmen detained in the United States or even allowing British creditors to sue American debtors for pre-Revolutionary debts, both unpopular clauses that many state governments chose to ignore with no legal consequences.

The *Treaty of Paris* provides the following:

"ALL PRISONERS ON BOTH SIDES SHALL BE SET AT LIBERTY, AND HIS BRITTANIC MAJESTY SHALL WITH ALL CONVENIENT SPEED, AND WITHOUT CAUSING ANY DESTRUCTION, OR CARRYING AWAY ANY NEGROES, OR OTHER PROPERTY OF THE AMERICAN INHABITANTS, WITHDRAW ALL HIS ARMIES, GARRISONS, AND FLEETS FROM THE SAID UNITED STATES, AND FROM EVERY POST, PLACE, AND HARBOR WITHIN THE SAME, LEAVING IN ALL FORTIFICATIONS, THE AMERICAN ARTILLERY THAT MAY BE THEREIN; AND SHALL ALSO ORDER AND CAUSE ALL ARCHIVE, RECORDS, DEEDS, AND PAPERS BELONGING TO ANY OF THE STATES, OR THEIR CITIZENS, WHICH IN THE COURSE OF THE WAR MAY HAVE FALLEN INTO THE HANDS OF HIS OFFICERS, TO BE FORTHWITH RESTORED AND DELIVERED TO THE PROPER STATES AND PERSONS TO WHOM THEY BELONG."

Many historians have observed that by envisioning the U.S. as a future major trading partner, the British imperial government had a statesmanlike perspective in finalizing the *Treaty of Paris* and made terms of the treaty extremely favorable to the United

States. The French foreign minister Charles Gravier, Count of Vergennes's assessment of the terms of the *Treaty of Paris* was "The English buy peace, rather than make it."

The delegates in the U.S. Congress were aware that the British imperial government viewed all Revolutionary War-era blacks as British subjects entitled to certificates of freedom under Article 7 of the treaty when it ratified the *Treaty of Paris* on January 14, 1784, at the Maryland Statehouse in Annapolis, Maryland. Under the treaty—black Englishmen were entitled to be "set at liberty," however, what became readily apparent was that despite the British imperial government's generosity and favorable terms granted to the U.S.—the power of the slave-holding members within the U.S. Congress and their wealthy constituency would never honor this agreed term within the treaty.

On paper, Congress had the power to regulate foreign affairs and could have asked slave-owning Americans throughout the 13 states to comply with the treaty's terms. Such could have been done—even though the *Articles* gave Congress no power to enforce its requests to the States. Arguably, a few—probably none of the slave-holding delegates in Congress would have voted to support such a resolution, which asked America's slave-holding citizenry to honor the solemnity of Congress's good-faith treaty ratification or for themselves to respect and honor their high office, thereby jeopardizing their wealth based upon colonial slavery; nonetheless, it was the duty of the Congress to try.

Being educated and Enlightened men—Congress knew black colonials were legally free people—having formally adopted Anglo-Saxon jurisprudence and England's common law in July 1776. Moreover, Congress knew with legal certainty that the 500,000 black Englishmen were all entitled to a due process hearing and knew the appropriate outcome. Granting black Englishmen—a due process hearing or any due process or honoring pre-Revolution obligations should have happened.

Supporting the notion of futility—Virginia passed a law refusing to honor payment of pre-Revolution debts to British creditors, which violated Article 4. In addition, all state governments violated Articles 5 and 6—regarding the return of confiscated loyalists' property. Thus, British forces continued occupying forts in the Great Lakes region, and these sovereign nations fought to resolve property rights violations under the treaty for years. However, denying due process and liberty to the 500,000 black Englishmen was provided for under Article 7, and U.S. Congress ignored their plight entirely.

The *Dred Scott* decision found:

"The only two clauses in the Constitution which point to this race treat them as persons whom it was morally lawfully to deal in as articles of property and to hold as slaves. . . ."

and

"The Constitution of the United States recognizes slaves as property and pledges the Federal Government to protect it. And Congress cannot exercise any more authority over property of that description than it may constitutionally exercise over property of any other kind. . . ."

After the *Treaty of Paris* that ended the Revolution was ratified, the U.S. did not confer unto the 500,000 black Englishmen suffering as slaves in America due process hearing to determine if such person was legally free or a slave. Yet, Taney found that any person of African ancestry could be dealt with "as articles of property and to hold as slaves. . . ."

Further, Taney "doubled down" by finding that the Framers of the Constitution, in his view, did not regard African Americans as being among the "people" for whose benefit and protection the new government was founded, notwithstanding the perfectly general language of the Declaration of Independence and the preamble to the Constitution. Moreover, Justice Benjamin R. Curtis of Massachusetts undercut most of Taney's historical arguments, showing that African Americans had voted in a number of states at the founding. "At the time of the ratification of the Articles of Confederation," he wrote:

"All free native-born inhabitants of the States of New Hampshire, Massachusetts, New York, New Jersey, and North Carolina, though descended from African slaves, were not only citizens of those States, but such of them as had the other necessary qualifications possessed the franchise of electors, on equal terms with other citizens." Concerning U.S. constitutions—the Framers of the *Articles of Confederation of 1777* did not have the power, and the Framers of its replacement in 1789 were color-conscious and never granted the 500,000 black Englishmen a due process hearing to determine if such people were legally free or slaves conclusively.

END NOTES

[1] Theodore R. Johnson, *How Conservatives Turned 'Color-Blind Constitution' Against Racial Progress*, The Atlantic, November 19, 2019

[2] *Dred Scott v. John A. Sandford*, 60 U. S. 393, 409 (1857) Indeed, it is "too clear for dispute," that the Declaration of Independence itself, when it declared that "all men are created equal," referred to whites and excluded blacks from the calculus. *See* id. at 410.

[3] Jerome M. Culp, Jr., *Colorblind Remedies and the Intersectionality of Oppression: Policy Arguments Masquerading as Moral Claims*, 69 N.Y.U.L. ReV. 162, 171 (1994) (noting that "the Constitution was, in modern constitutional parlance, facially neutral while protecting racial subjugation by private parties and even government entities.")

[4] The *Magna Carta*, issued by King John in 1215, is the foundation of the unwritten British constitution. It established guarantees of trial by jury and habeas corpus, and generally protected the citizenry's well-being from those ruling. The vagueness of the document has caused many over the centuries to interpret it differently, but its importance in being the basis for Western democracy is unquestioned.

[5] A. V. Dicey, Introduction to the Study of the Law of the Constitution, (1885)

[6] Sir Thomas Smith, *De Republica Anglorum, A Discourse o the Commonwealth of England*, Book II, chapter 1, L. Alston (ed), with an introduction by F.W. Maitland, CUP (1906)

[7] The English monarch and imperial government controlled the upper house, and under the colonial

charter, Virginia's 1662 hereditary slavery resolution required the King's assent to become law. Moreover, the pretended hereditary slave law of Virginia's colonial assembly conflicted with England's *Magna Carta of 1215* prohibiting slavery and the common law doctrine of *partus sequitur patrem,* which established that the father's condition defined the legal status of a child born in the colony of Virginia.

[8] Arthur Meier Schlesinger, *Colonial Appeals to the Privy Council,* Political Science Quarterly, Vol. 28, No. 3 (Sep. 193), pp. 433-450... Colonial appeals to the Privy Council concerning the enactment hereditary slave laws and changing the patrilineal descend system for people of African descent were within the fixed classes of enactment, i.e. (1) colonial charters and (2) laws passed by colonial assemblies. The ability to appeal to the *Privy Council* secured important advantages to colonists, as it represented a means of relief from arbitrary proceedings of colonial courts and colonial assemblies.

[9] Robert A. Ferguson, *The American Enlightenment: 1750-1820* (Cambridge: Harvard University Press, 1994; paperback ed. 1997

[10] Alan Taylor, American Colonies: The Settling of North America (Viking/Penguin, 2001)

[11] Julius Goebel, *Antecedents and Beginnings To 1801, History of The Supreme Court of the Unites States,* observed that the concept of judicial review was operative during colonial times as the British *Privy Council* was an intermediary appellate tribunal to review colonial legislation.

[12] *James Somerset v. Charles Stewart*, (K.B. 1772)

[13] The first hub and spoke conspiracy case in the U.S. did not use the term hub-and-spoke. See *Interstate Circuit v. U.S.*, 306 U.S. 208 (1939). A later loan fraud

conspiracy used the metaphor of a hub and spoke of a wheel, while finding there was no actual "rim" or horizontal agreement. *Kotteakos v. United States*, 328 U.S. 750, 756 (1946) (finding that without horizontal agreements among the rim parties, there may be multiple conspiracies, but not one unifying conspiracy).

[14] The First Circuit Court of Appeals of the United States observed that "in a 'hub-and-spoke conspiracy,' a central mastermind, or 'hub' controls numerous 'spokes,' or secondary co-conspirators. These co-conspirators participate in independent transactions with the individual or group of individuals at the 'hub' that furthers a single, illegal enterprise.

[15] Section II of the *Declaratory Act* provided: "And be it further declared and enacted by the authority aforesaid, That all resolutions, votes, orders, proceedings, in any of the said colonies or plantations, whereby the power and authority of the parliament, whereby the power and authority of the parliament of Great Britain, to make laws and statutes as aforesaid is denied, or drawn into question, arc, and are hereby declared to be, utterly null and void to all in purposes whatsoever."

[16] J. A. Guy, *Origin of the Petition of Right Reconsidered*, The Historical Journal, p. 289-312, (1982)

[17] Micheal Kenny, Alison L. Young, *Constitutional Entrenchment and Parliamentary Sovereignty*, Institute for Government-Bennett Institute for Public Policy, Review of the UK Constitution Guest Paper (2023)

[18] Legally, villeins ranked between free labourers and unfree chattel slaves. Villeins occupied a plot of land on a manor in exchange for their labor. They took an oath of Fealty to the owner of the manor.

[19] Larry Kenneth Alexander, *Smoke, Mirrors, and Chains: America's First Continuing Criminal Enterprise*, Trafford Pub., ISBN 978-1-4907-6833-5 (2016)
[20] Alan Taylor, American Colonies (New York: Viking) (2001), p. 213.
[21] Ibid. at p. 156.
[22] Larry Kenneth Alexander, *Smoke, Mirrors, and Chains: America's First Continuing Criminal Enterprise*, Trafford Pub., ISBN 978-1-4907-6833-5 (2016), prologue p. xvi.
[23] *America Past and Present Online—The Laws of Virginia (1662, 1691, 1705)* Archived 2008-04-21 at the Wayback Machine
[24] Alan Taylor, American Colonies (New York: Viking) (2001), p. 156.
[25] Betty Wood, *Origins of American Slavery,* Macmillan: Hill and Wang Critical Issues Series, ISBN 9780809016082, (1997) p. 92.
[26] Larry Kenneth Alexander, *The Case for Liberty: The Criminal Enslavement of Colonial Englishmen*, Amazon Pub., ISBN 979-8-8331-09663 (2022)
[27] Micheal Kenny, *Constitutional Entrenchment and Parliamentary Sovereignty: Review of the UK Guest Paper*, Bennett Institute for Public Policy, Institute for Government (2023)
[28] The *Declaratory Act* was not repealed during colonial times, and as all colonial hereditary slave statutes and slave laws, resolutions, votes, orders, and related proceedings were abolished in 1766—hereditary slavery was not a legally authorized practice in colonial America in July 1776.
[29] See, for example, Mary Sarah Bilder, *The Transatlantic Constitution: Colonial Legal Culture and the Empire* (Cambridge, MA: Harvard University Press, 2004) and Daniel J. Hulsebosch, Constituting Empire: New York and

the Transformation of Constitutionalism in the Atlantic World, 1664-1830 (Chapel Hill: UNC Press, 2006).
[30] The practice of reserving cases for twelve-judges deliberation began in the 18th century, but only a handful appeared before the 1770s—all with Mansfield. Prior to the late 18th century, there was no regular printed record of the twelve-judge procedure. Occasionally, twelve-judge cases turned up in the nominative reports, and trial records in a few seminal cases printed in pamphlet form.
[31] James Oldham, *Informal Law-Making in England by the Twelve Judges in the late 18th and early 19th Centuries*, 27 Law & History Rev. (2011)
[32] Paul Finkelman, *Dred Scott v. Sandford: A Brief History with Documents*, (Boston: Bedford Books, 1997)
[33] Self-executing in law refers to the immediate effectiveness of things such as legislation, contracts without any required court action.
[34] *R. (Miller) v. Secretary of State for Exiting the European Union* [2017} UKSC 5., [2018] 1 AX 61; *R. (Miller) v. The Prime Minister; Cherry v. Advocate General for Scotland* [2019] UKSC 41, [2020] AC 373.
[35] Further, the textbook definition of the British State and the doctrine of parliamentary sovereignty is set-forth in A. V. Dicey's book *Introduction to the Law of the Constitution 1885*. . . "Unitarianism, in short, means the concentration of the strength of the State in the hands of one visible sovereign power, be that Parliament or Czar."
[36] Dickinson's *Letter from a Farmer* "first appeared in a dozen installments in a Philadelphia newspaper between December 1767 and February 1768 [and] was ultimately printed in twenty-one of the twenty-five colonial newspapers."

[37] Ibid.
[38] Ibid.
[39] Ibid., 4 June, 1766
[40] Consequently, Acts of Parliament cannot be struck down as unconstitutional by the courts. There is, however, one limit on parliament's power. It cannot enact legislation that would bind a future parliament, either as to the content of legislation or as to the manner in which legislation is made. Were any one parliament to attempt to do so, it would always be possible for a future parliament to reverse this requirement. That is the principle of parliamentary sovereignty, as traditionally understood.
[41] "What Was the British Policy of Salutary Neglect? *historyofmassachusetts.org.* Retrieved 2020-02-09
[42] *Constitutional Entrenchment and Parliamentary Sovereignty*, p. 4.
[43] Guy Chet, *The Colonists' American Revolution*, John Wiley & Sons, (2019)
[44] *Dr. Bonham's Case* (K.B. 1610)
[45] During colonial times—a pretended statute or law—enacted in excess of power or an unconstitutional provision of an act is void *ab initio*. That is, they are inoperative as if they had never been passed. Void means without legal effect. *Ab initio* is a Latin term meaning "from the beginning"; therefore, void *ab initio* means an action that never had legal effect. A void "act," "statute," or "law" that was done without jurisdiction cannot be rectified to become enforceable because it is deemed as though it never occurred. The parties are placed in their original positions.
[46] *James Somerset v. Charles Stewart*, (K.B. 1772)

[47] *The Five Knights Case* also called Darnel's Case, 3 How St. Tr. 1 (K.B. 1627)

[48] All slavery statutes and laws passed by colonial assemblies within the American colonies were void *ab initio*.

[49] Donald Yacovone, *Teaching White Supremacy: America's Democratic Ordeal and the Forging of Our National Identity,* Pantheon Books, ISBN 978-0-593-31663-4 (2020) The Massachusetts Supreme Court in *Roberts v. City of Boston*, 59 Mass. (5.Cush.) 198 (1850) ruled that local elected officials had the authority to control local schools did not violate black students' rights. The decision was cited over and over again in later cases to justify segregation.

[50] *American Colonies Act 1766* also known as *Declaratory Act of 1766*.

[51] John M. Murrin, Paul E. Johnson, James M. McPherson, Alice Fahs, Gary Gerstle, *Liberty, Equality, Power: A History of the American People, Volume 1 To 1877,* Concise Edition, Cengage Learning, ISBN 9781285657516 (2013)

[52] David Leon Ammerman, *In the Common Cause: American Response to the Coercive Acts of 1774*, ISBN 978-08113905259 (1974) While many sources claim that the *Quartering Act* allowed British troops to be billeted in occupied private homes, historian David Ammerman's 1974 study claimed this is a myth, and that the act only permitted troops to be quartered in unoccupied buildings. *id*. p. 10

[53] Benson John Lossing, *Our Country: A Household History for All Readers, from the Discovery of America to the Present Time, Volume 3*, Appendix Amies Pub. Co. (1888)

[54] *Plessy v. Ferguson*, 163 U. S. 537, 559 (1896) (Harlan, J., dissenting), Writing his famous dissent, Justice Harlan stated, "The Constitution of the United States does not, I think, permit any public authority the right to know the race of those entitled to be protected in the enjoyment of those rights." *Id*. at 554. In a frequently quoted passage, Harlan later stated, "Our Constitution is color-blind and neither knows nor tolerates classes among citizens." *Id*. at 559.
[55] U.S. CONST. amend. XIII
[56] U. S. CONST. amend. XIV
[57] U. S. CONST. amend. XV
[58] Congressman Thaddeus Stevens proposed the following language based on the original ideas of Wendell Philips): "All national and State laws shall be equally applicable to every citizen and no discrimination shall be made on account of race or color." Andrew Kull, *The Color-Blind Constitution vii*. But, Congressman Bingham's counterproposal of "equal protection" carried the day. See *id*.at 87.
[59] Laurence Tribe, *In What Vision of the Constitution Must the Law Be Color-Blind?* 20 J. Marshall L. REV. 201, 204 (citing Alexander M. Bickel, *The Original Understanding and the Segregation Decision*, 69 HARV. L. REV. 1, 56 (1955) ("We know, with as much certainty as such matters ever permit, that the Framers of the Fourteenth Amendment did not think "equal protection of the laws" made all racial distinctions in law unconstitutional; they did not intend, for example to outlaw racially segregated public schools").
[60] See *Plessy*, 163 U. S. at 542. Justice Brown held that a law which recognized the color of the two races did not destroy their legal equality or reestablish involuntary servitude. Id at 543.

[61] Ibid. Later, Justice Brown added that any such interpretation would be "solely because the colored race chooses to put that construction upon it." Id at 551. Justice Brown supported his position by noting the constitutionality of separate schools for white and black children and laws forbidding racial intermarriages. See i. at 544-55.

[62] *Regents of University of California v. Bakke*, 438 U. S. 265, 401 (1978) (Marshall, J. concurring in part and dissenting in part) ("From *Plessy* to *Brown v. Board of Education*, ours was a Nation where, by law, an individual could be given "special treatment" based on the color of his skin".)

[63] Mary K. Geiter, William Arthur Speck, *Colonial America From Jamestown to Yorktown*, Macmillan New York 2002

[64] Eric Foner, *Give Me Liberty: An American History* (New York: W.W. Norton & Company, 2009, p. 100

[65] Theodore W. Allen, *The Invention of the White Race: Racial Oppression and Social Control*, New Expanded Edition, VersoBooks (2012)

[66] Murray Newton Rothbard and Leonard P. G. Liggio, *Conceived in Liberty*, Vol. I, Arlington Pub, House (1975)

[67] Not only did these slave resolutions, votes, orders, and proceedings override and set aside the legislation of Parliament, but they were also in conflict with England's common law doctrines of *jus soli* and *partus sequitur patrem*—declaring that the legal status of a child born in the Kingdom was that of a freeborn Englishman and a patrilineal descent system. Hereditary slavery was the product of this criminal conspiracy, which became endemic throughout the American colonies and was principally why colonial assemblies began ignoring

Parliament's *Royal Assent by Commission Act of 1541* and the *Sedition Act of 1661.*

[68] Putative colonial slave statutes and laws promulgated by colonial assemblies without Parliament's assent and formal blessing challenged the Parliament's exclusive "power and authority" to make laws in the Kingdom. This suggestion and conclusion are given weight in the grievance section of the Declaration of Independence... which labels King George III as a tyrant for, among many other allegations, *"abolishing our most valuable laws..."* And if "abolishing" of colonial laws was not accomplished by this section of the Act—the question is raised, what Act of the British imperial government caused the abolishment of colonial laws *before* the Declaration of Independence, as the Founding Generation claimed.

[69] The textbook analysis of the British State and the doctrine of parliamentary sovereignty is set-forth in A. V. Dicey's book *Introduction to the Law of the Constitution 1885.* . . "Unitarianism, in short, means the concentration of the strength of the State in the hands of one visible sovereign power, be that Parliament or Czar."

[70] David Armitage, *The Declaration of Independence: A Global History*, Cambridge, Massachusetts: Harvard University Press (2007)

[71] Francis D. Cogliano, *Thomas Jefferson: Reputation and Legacy*, Edinburgh University Press, ISBN 978-0748624997 2008, p. 219; Peter S. Onuf, *The Mind of Thomas Jefferson*, University of Virginia Press, ISBN 978-0813926117, 2007, p. 258

[72] Joseph Ellis, *American Sphinx*, Alfred A. Knopf, ISBN 978-0679444909, 1997, p. 87

[73] Thomas J. DiLorenzo, *Yankee Confederates: New England Secession Movement Prior to the War Between the States,"* in David Gordon, ed., *Secession, State and Liberty,* Transaction Publishers, 1998
[74] Henry Wiencek, *Master of the Mountain: Thomas Jefferson and His Slaves*, Macmillan, 2012, pp. 114, 122
[75] Alfred W. Blumrosen, Ruth G. Blumrosen, *Slave Nation: How Slavery United the Colonies and Sparked the American Revolution*, Naperville, Illinois: Sourcebooks, Inc. (2005)
[76] This interpretation is supported by William M. Wiecek, Somerset Case being referenced in the treatise, *Encyclopedia of the American Constitution* by scholars Leonard W. Levy and Kenneth L. Karst, eds. New York: Macmillan Reference USA 2000, Vol. 5, pp. 2452, where they concluded that "because the precent had become part of American common law."
[77] David Leon Ammerman, *In the Common Cause: American Response to the Coercive Acts of 1774*, ISBN 978-0813905259 (1974)
[78] Edmund S. Morgan, *American Slavery, American Freedom: The Ordeal of Colonial Virginia*, W.W. Norton & Company, New York (1975)
[79] Alfred and Ruth G. Blumrosen, *Slave Nation: How Slavery United the Colonies and Parked the American Revolution*, Naperville; Sourcebooks Inc. (2005)
[80] *James Somerset v. Charles Stewart*, (K.B. 1772)
[81] George van Cleve, *Somerset Case and its Antecedents in Imperial Perspective*, Law and History Review 24.3 (2006); Dana Rabin, *Empire on Trial; Slavery, Villeinage and Law in Imperial Britain*; in Legal Histories of the British Empire, ed. Shaunnagh Dorsett and John McLaren (New York, 2014), p. 205
[82] *Rex v. Stapyton* (K. B. 1771)

[83] *Smith v. Gould,* 2 Ld. Raym. 1274-75; 92 Eng. Rep. 499 (Q. B. 1706)
[84] Lawrence Goldstone, *Inherently Unequal: The Betrayal of Equal Rights by the Supreme Court, 1865-1903*, Walker & Company (2011) p. 23-24
[85] Melvin Urofsky, *Dred Scott Decision* | Definition, History, Summary, Significance, & Facts | Britannica, Encyclopedia Britannica (2023) "Among constitutional scholars, *Scott v. Sandford* is widely considered the worst decision ever rendered by the Supreme Court. It has been cited in particular, as the most egregious example in the court's history of wrongly imposing a judicial solution on a political problem. A later chief justice, Charles Evans Hughes, famously characterized the decision as the court's great "self-inflicted wound."
[86] Leonard Ricards, *Shays' Rebellion: The American Revolution's Final Battle*, Philadelphia: University of Pennsylvania Press, 2002

www.ingramcontent.com/pod-product-compliance
Lightning Source LLC
LaVergne TN
LVHW011415080426
835512LV00005B/77